ARABANA AND THE GHAN

MICHAEL DUKE

ARABANA AND THE GHAN

WITH AN INTRODUCTION BY AARON STUART

Connor Court Publishing

Published in 2019 by Connor Court Publishing Pty Ltd

Copyright © Michael Duke 2019

All rights reserved. No part of this book may be reproduced or transmitted in any form or by any means, electronic or mechanical, including photocopying, recording or by any information storage and retrieval system, without prior permission in writing from the publisher.

Connor Court Publishing Pty Ltd

PO Box 7257

Redland Bay QLD 4165

sales@connorcourt.com

www.connorcourtpublishing.com.au

Phone 0497 900 685

ISBN: 9781925826289

Front Cover Design: Maria Giordano

Front Cover Photo: "Water Tower and Steam Train" by Sue Dodd.

Printed in Australia

DEDICATION

To the Arabana people of the south west and including Kati Thanda/Lake Eyre, wherever they may now be, and Elders past and present.

Warning:

Deceased Aboriginal persons are discussed and depicted in these pages.

TABLE OF CONTENTS

Foreword	1
Acknowledgements	11
Introduction by Arabana Elder, Aaron Stuart	13
Preamble	15
Definitions	21
Chapter 1 - A Review of Some Important Issues	25
Chapter 2 - Living in "The Desert": Australia's Red Heart	43
Chapter 3 - From Songlines to Trainlines	77
Chapter 4 - Arabana on the Railway	107
Chapter 5 - Arabana Rail Workers and Their Families: Their Stories	123
Chapter 6 - Arabana Making History	189
Appendix 1: Railways and Other Indigenous People in Australia: The Age of Steam Enters The Dreaming	197
Appendix 2: Some Arabana Rail Workers Names	221
Timeline	225
References	231

FOREWORD

This book is about the old Ghan and the Arabana Aboriginal people from Northern South Australia from 1884 to 1983. The Ghan is the railway that now links Adelaide and Darwin. This link, however, is only a recent development. For nearly a hundred years the railway line extended only from Adelaide to Alice Springs. For the Arabana, the railway offered opportunities which were not available to most other Aboriginal peoples, who were usually only able to work on sheep or cattle stations or live in Missions. The Arabana helped survey, construct, work upon and service the railway from its beginnings in 1884. By the 1930s, many Arabana were employed in skilled occupations and had wage parity with white workers. The railway also provided the Arabana with opportunities to travel beyond their country and into settler society, without losing their own culture. This book has stories from Arabana themselves who have worked upon the railway or had relatives who did so.

ACKNOWLEDGEMENTS

So many people have helped this book come to fruition. Reg Dodd, of Arabunna Aboriginal Tours, introduced me to the idea of Arabana benefitting from the Railways. I am especially grateful to all the people who agreed to be interviewed and have their stories appear. Professor Veronica Arbon, Arabana Academic, was very kind and helpful and introduced me to her wonderful family. And I thank Aaron Stuart, former head of Ularaka, now Arabana Aboriginal Corporation, for undertaking the task of providing an introduction from the Arabana people.

Also thanks are due to the staff of the National Australian Archives in Canberra and Sydney, the State Records of South Australia, State Librarians in South Australia, the helpful librarians at AIATSIS, the staff of the Coinda Centre in Port Augusta, Geraldine Mate of the Ipswich Railway Workshops Museum and William Watt, Manager, Land Tenure and Statutory Support, Development Division, Department of Planning, Transport and Infrastructure, South Australia. Malcolm McKinnon, film-maker, whose six short films about Arabana were very enlightening. Luise Hercus, distinguished linguist of ANU, gave me much time and several volumes, including a comprehensive Arabana vocabulary. Greg Wilson, linguist, was very humorous and full of insights. Mick Garrett patiently drew the several versions of the map. John Mannion, railway historian and Deane Fergie gave me useful tips. Especially for many many hours over the past four years, my supervisor for the Monash University thesis, Dr Tom Heenan.

Visits to the National Railway Museum Adelaide and the Ghan

Railway Museums in Oodnadatta and Alice Springs were illuminating and indispensable.

My editor Susan SP Dodd has been untiring in seeking to improve the quality and readability of the book. Enormous thanks for all her efforts. Any residual errors are my own.

Finally, my wife Margaret who travelled with me throughout Arabana country and met many of the Arabana people along the way. She has been encouraging and ably helping at all stages.

INTRODUCTION

ARABANA ELDER, AARON STUART

18th August 2015

Aaron is currently working at Centacare, Port Augusta. I wish to thank Aaron for writing this introduction and for his time and interest. As well as the interview which occurs later in the book, he also allowed me several conversations and gave me and my wife Margaret a driving tour of Finniss Springs with commentary in 2014.

Mike Duke

"Hello every one my name is Aaron Clayton STUART, I am the son of Rex STUART who has passed away about 15 years ago, currently I am the Arabana Chair and have been for the past 8 years, My grandfather Laurie Stuart was one of the original Native title claimants for the Arabana, he also was traditional cultured man who knew a lot of our customs along with being born and raised in the bush, he too has passed away leaving knowledge only to a select few.

I am honoured to write about the Arabana People (Tribe) to describe how important they were into opening up one of the most harshest environment in the world "the Australia's outback" showing the early explorers and the Afghan Camel trains where water could be found along the sacred paths of the Dreaming Stories that sustained Arabana people for over 40 thousand years leading into the National Railway line thru to Alice Springs in the Northern Territory.

It would be a fair comment to explore the actual life forces that was hidden from many except the Australian Aboriginal only to be found in many Aboriginal tribes stories and song lines creating a path that opened a continent from South to North by the giving water of life, these are the mound springs.

In Arabana country these mound springs are in large volumes sustaining a way of life that was before the Afghan cameleers, pastoralist and the early explorers. The Arabana were connected to this land not for the riches of wealth, money, pastoralism or minerals but to live a way of life that connect them to the earth with an animistic focus that prolonged a greater life expectancies in harmony. This came to an end with the introduction with aristocratic style of ownership from a system that never had the right to claim or take land in the beginning, many times using harsh methods to rid of the Arabana people this included policy and death after being showed the life giving outlets from this large land. When it was realised that this great resource of water was underground and could develop this nation the Arabana simply fell or placed into system that would always oppress them and provide a second class life than what they had using them for what they could do and knew, once this action was completed the remaining Arabana were absorbed into a European Western way of working life mainly on cattle station and the Railways that ran straight thru their land.

Some not many would become great employees to the Railways and the rest would fall back in the new Australian society that treated them different and always changed with the evolution of education and service delivery that seemed to be totally different from the dream time. Away of long ago is slowly being lost like the railways to a new ever changing land scape that covers all spectrums of life innovative change that the Arabana find it hard to keep up".

Aaron Stuart

PREAMBLE

"The past is a foreign country.
They do things differently there"
L.P. Hartley (1953)

The Arabana had a different history and opportunities to other Aboriginal groups because of the railway. But this is not only a history of the Arabana's contribution. The book also shows that the railway was directly influenced by the Arabana themselves. They were actively involved in linking Australia's southern cities with the centre and latterly northern cities. In this they helped "over-write" the song lines running from Port Augusta to the Tiwi Islands with that revolutionary technology, the railway. They engaged in ways quite different to the near-feudal pastoral industry, and were paid equal wages from 1927 onwards, quite different to most other Aboriginal workers in other industries, and occurring forty years before the Equal Wage case of the 1960s. For instance, the basic wage in 1965 was fifteen pounds and eighteen shillings a week. According to Gale, writing in 1964, of 32 Aboriginal stockmen employed on a northern pastoral station, only three were paid the basic wage. White stockmen usually got more. Sixteen Aboriginal stockmen got half the basic wage while the rest got even less.

Arabana still live predominantly up and down the old railway line from Darwin to Adelaide and have gained Native Title for much of their traditional country. Twenty-first century Arabana are now involved with the ecological changes associated with global climate change, with green energy projects and re-greening their own country, as well as proselytising about uranium mining and other diverse issues.

Running through their country are the remnants of the Old Ghan line which continues to fascinate people. With the Overland Telegraph, which also traverses Arabana country, the Old Ghan is one of the great infrastructure projects in this nation's history and was among the world's iconic rail journeys. It has not only linked the country' southern cities to the centre and the north, but has also been crucial in the nation's economic development and defence.

The commemorative "Anzac Ghan" runs annually from Adelaide to Darwin, commemorating the 20,000 or so troops who took that route to defend Australia during World War II against the likelihood of a Japanese invasion. The "Anzac Ghan" trip not only contributes to the region's tourism sector, but highlights the national importance of the railway line. The trip includes historical talks on board, a side trip on an old steam train, the Pichi Richi Railway, which travels a part of the Old Ghan line from Port Augusta to Quorn. The ANZAC Ghan is the subject of a Photo Essay in The Outback Magazine (Issue 94, May/ June 2014, pp76-81).

Many tourists travel the iconic Oodnadatta Track. This parallels the Old Ghan route much of the way and was originally the service road for the railway. Museums dedicated to the Old Ghan exist in Alice Springs and Oodnadatta. Old buildings such as railway stations have been converted into restaurants, telecommunications centres and so on. A couple of fettlers' cottages, spaced every 16 kilometres along the track, are still in reasonable condition, although more could be done to preserve or restore them. Signage about the "Ghan Trail" is ubiquitous whilst celebration of the people who helped construct and maintained the railway line and its trains has been lacking. Hidden within this history is the story of the Arabana who were involved in all stages of the railway's development.

This book starts with a discussion on the development of the railways and how they were perceived as emblematic of both Western civilization and the British Empire's progress. The first chapter also explores how such views tried to justify the conquest and dispossession of Indigenous peoples, and the proliferation of race-based theories to support the latter's exclusion from so-called white, civilized societies. Throughout the nineteenth century, the railway was a central symbol of the perceived superiority of the British over lesser races. Yet stories of Aboriginal involvement with the railways have rarely been told. Through Arabana stories it becomes clear that the railway provided them with the opportunities denied to more remotely located Indigenous peoples.

In June 2011 I travelled to the Tiwi Islands where the significance of the Ghan to Aboriginal peoples became even more evident. In Nguiu, the capital of the Tiwi Islands, it was the day before they celebrated the 100th Anniversary of the arrival of Bishop Gsell, the priest who converted many to Christianity, but left substantial aspects of the traditional culture intact. There is a Dreaming track which runs all the way from the Tiwi Islands to Port Augusta. It runs basically north to south near the route the train line had followed from the 1860s to 1980, and was associated with the "native cat", the quoll.

Among the various events, the Tiwi Islanders performed a smoking ceremony to ensure that no evil spirits came with the tourists onto the Island. Later they showed local dances. Dancing or *yoi* is a part of everyday life on the Tiwi islands. The Tiwi Islanders inherit their totemic dance from their mother. Different dances are performed for different reasons. Some spontaneously happen at celebrations as an expression of emotion, while others occur in a more structured manner at ceremonies.

Narrative dances are performed and can depict everyday life or historical events. The bombing of Darwin in the Second World War has been portrayed through Indigenous song and dance, as have many other significant events. Singing always accompanies dancing and new songs are continually being created. The dances performed for my tour group in 2011 were entitled Shark, Crocodile, Buffalo (from the water buffalo introduced by the British in 1824) and Battleship (from World War 2 when the Tiwi fought so bravely against the Japanese). Then the Islanders preformed a farewell Train Dance to the tour group. But there are no trains on the Tiwi Islands and never have been. The Tiwi guide said about the origins of the dance "Oh, it's the Ghan. Our people went to the mainland and saw and travelled on the train. We brought it back as a dance".

Clearly the train, the Ghan, is as memorable as a Japanese battleship! A huge war machine and a train each had their perhaps antithetical stories told. And the train's impression upon the observant Tiwi people was worth remembering and transmitting to the whole Tiwi population. The Dance seemed to show emotional greetings and farewells of connected people, and to me represented the scenes one sees so often in old movies, when a train journey was the start or end of a relationship. A local Indigenous culture had incorporated the Train into its own idiom to bid farewell.

Physical and social mobility are outcomes of the railways. Arabana capitalised on this, moving from their traditional culture to pastoral serfdom, then to casual, then to permanent work on the railway. They adapted, by gaining an education in Western literacy and numeracy, to win promotions and further opportunities in the dominant white society. Their descendants are now gaining tertiary education and employment in trades and profession outside Arabana country but also have opportunities to re-assert aspects of their traditional culture. As this book shows, the railway has been central to these developments. E.M Forster was moved to write about railways, "They are our gates to the glorious and the unknown" (in Williams, 2005, p240).

Service personnel at Oodnadatta, labelled by the photographer as 'cattle - 1st class to Darwin'. Approximately 1945

Photograph Courtesy of the State Library of South Australia [PRG 1435/4/6]

DEFINITIONS

Conductor: term used in other countries for a guard.

Fireman: person who, in a steam locomotive, tends the furnace which powers the engine.

Ganger: person in charge of a gang, five or more workers, plus a cook, who travelled the railway line doing maintenance and repairs. They often lived in tents: "the flying gang" or more permanent gangs had houses at 15 Km intervals up and down the line. Some of the houses survive; most along the old Ghan line have been trashed.

Guard: person who travels on and ensures the safety of the train, its passengers and freight as it travels the length of the railway line. He or she carries out control and information activities on the train. A guard monitors the carriages or trucks of the train and their equipment, checking on possible defects that might jeopardise the safety of the operation. A guard may check the tickets and issue supplementary fare tickets in passenger trains. He or she may provide information on routes and travel times. He or she can check the lighting and heating in carriages.

Locomotive Engineer: steam engine driver.

Navvy, Fettler: railway track worker, these workers install and maintain railway tracks, as well as the tracks that are used in quarries and by the mining industry. They lay and fix the foundations and sleepers for tracks, cut rails to length, install railway switches, and repair and maintain worn or rough rail ends. They can be welders of track. They remove damaged track parts, examine and maintain switch signal lamps and the wheel bearings of rolling stock, and may also assist with the righting of derailed rolling stock. Railway track workers work in both the passenger and freight rail service industries and are therefore required all over the state, from the busy passenger lines to freight lines.

Train Examiner: person who inspects rolling stock in railway yards, terminals and stations to ensure adherence to safety standards and operational rules and regulations.

Yardmaster: this occupation is responsible for overseeing the operations of a rail yard and assigning duties to workers. These duties include placing and pulling carriages and wagons, switching inbound or outbound traffic, reviewing train schedules, moving railcars, performing inspections and making repairs. Yardmasters ensure that all cargo and railcars safely reach their intended destinations in a timely fashion. They must be aware of any train or rail problems, and plan alternate routes as necessary.

Section Car: Also known as an inspection car or tuk-tuk, this is a small vehicle used to move rail workers quickly between sites upon the train line. The old section cars were belt driven and were nicknamed "red birds"; later ones had a motor. It was faster than the old hand-car. Some only had three wheels although most had four.

Budd Car: A self-propelled diesel rail car, often silver when used on the Old Ghan. Sometimes they had another rail car attached. They came into use once Standard Gauge was put through to Marree in 1957.

Carbine: a NSU class diesel locomotive.

Pay Car : White painted pay cars for workers' salaries and wages were attached to some trains. One end was fitted up as a paymaster's office. Next to the office was a space with two longitudinal berths. The remainder of the car was fitted with tables, a shower and one toilet.

Railway employees at Callanna Railway Station near Marree
(Photograph Courtesy of the State Library of South Australia B-54698-26)

1

A REVIEW OF SOME IMPORTANT ISSUES

"There is no document of civilisation which is not at the same time a document of barbarism" – Walter Benjamin (1969)

The Arabana people's contribution to the pioneering and development of the Australian nation has not been told. Their knowledge and labour were crucial to the extension and servicing of communication links between Australia's south and north. As the original inhabitants of the country around the west, south and north of Lake Eyre/Kati Thanda (Arabana name reclaimed 2013), the Arabana have been important contributors to the surveying, construction, working upon and servicing the rail link from Adelaide to Alice Springs. It is time to put Arabana's contribution 'back on the train' in Australian history.

This chapter encompasses the idea of progress, which involves valuing novelty, some comments upon race theory and its impact upon colonisation, some transport history, "corridor theory", labour history and Aboriginal history. Arabana men and women working upon the railway come out of the shadows and assume their rightful place in this narrative. The contribution of Aboriginal pastoral workers have become increasingly recognised, as is covered below, but their position has been portrayed as subordinate, almost serf-like or enslaved. The Indigenous contribution to railways was different.

The Empire, Railways and the Idea of Progress

This book adds to the information about the connections between Aboriginal peoples, the white settlers and the revolutionary progressive technology of the railway. Railways were seen as emblematic of progress: "the age of steam" is a metonym for nearly the entire nineteenth century, where steamships, railways and factory machines like the Spinning Jenny built the Industrial Revolution. The idea of "progress", that things new and revolutionary are desirable, emerged especially during the Industrial Revolution. The Enlightenment era from the early seventeenth to the early nineteenth century saw an explosion of such technological innovations, which were perceived as liberating for humanity from labour-intensive drudgery and helplessness before the powers of nature. Trevithick's and Watt's steam engines were invented by the end of the eighteenth century. This was accompanied by colonisation by the rising Western powers of many areas of the world. This book acknowledges that British settlers appropriated Aboriginal land and substituted their animals and crops for those already in existence and utilised in the country.

Throughout most of the era of colonisation of Australia, Western thinking held that so-called "primitive" peoples, usually marked by different skin colouration, were inferior to "Occidentals". And it was during this time, when the Western world valued "progress" above all, that steam railways, the Iron Horse, the "Age of Steam", were brought to Australia in the 1850s. Arabana challenged that inferiority notion as the railway moved into their country. The idea of progress is often a part of the histories of the European powers. By way of contrast, the Indian-origin academic Sengoopta (2003) writes rather scoffingly: "Every schoolchild knows that Britain gave its colonies the railway and the telegraph. It is recalled rather less often that it got curry, fingerprinting and Worcestershire sauce in return, each of which has outlived the telegraph and, given the state of things in today's Britain, might even outlast the railway" (p6).

The British Empire evolved rapidly over the nineteenth century. Adam Smith writing in 1776 called British society, as it operated then, the "project of an empire"; it was embryonic, nascent, but not yet realised. By the mid nineteenth century the project had become not just an empire, but the British Empire, upon which the sun never set. Perhaps the defining moment of this emergence is when Britain assumed direct control of India after the 1857 so-called Sepoy Mutiny. John Darwin in his 2009 book, *The Empire Project*, suggests this "British world-system", as he calls it, rested on three pillars: naval and military superiority; the commercial power of the City of London, and rapid communications. Darwin also notes the importance of British migration: one in six inhabitants of the British Isles emigrated between 1830 and 1870 to their various colonies. But the glue which held this sprawling empire together was the communication systems. These included the telegraph, steamship and the railway, linking British colonies to the metropole, London, and to each other.

Settler colonisation of Australia entailed philosophical, religious, political, legal, agricultural and population based arguments and ideas. To achieve their freedom from ideas embedding racial prejudice against Indigenous peoples in general, the Arabana used their involvement with that epitome of modernity, the railway. Fortunately, the north of South Australia had relatively benign landholders, unlike some areas. By way of contrast, the Gadubanud, King Parrot people, of the Cape Otway area in Victoria were basically exterminated to ensure the safety of the Lighthouse Keepers.

The philosophy of "race" seemed to start latterly being expressed with the idea, articulated by Thomas Hobbes in *Leviathan* (1651), that groups of humans naturally competed and had lives nasty, brutish and short. The Spanish theologian and academic Francisco de Vitoria of Salamanca University had earlier contested the ideas of racial superiority and the morality of colonisation but Hobbes and his successors prevailed in that later era. That Europeans as the "superior race" undertook colonisation and overran so-called "inferior" cultures was considered natural, inevitable and unlikely to change. From the time of Columbus onwards, the sixteenth century, there was promoted the idea of a hierarchy of human beings with Europeans being at the top and other "races" in descending order below. This view was expressed by English explorer and pirate William Dampier (1729, p 464), for instance, who wrote of Northern Australia "The inhabitants of this country are the miserablest People in the world. The Hodmadods of Monomatapa, though a nasty people, yet for wealth are gentlemen to these; who have no houses and skin garments, sheep, poultry and fruits of the earth, ostrich eggs &c. as the Hodmadods have: and setting aside their humane shape, they differ but little from brutes."

Clothing, housing, agriculture, and animal husbandry are seen by Dampier as the hallmarks of superior culture. This notion is strangely echoed in the foundation document for South Australia *(South Australia Act, 1834)*, whereby being clothed, participating in agriculture, living in houses and being converted to the truths of Christianity are stated directly and enjoined upon the Aborigines.

Within this hierarchy of "race", once "discovered" by the Western powers, Aboriginal Australians were seen as the bottom of the chain. They were conceived of as relics, as people who had not "progressed" *(my inverted commas)*, from the Europeans' Stone Age and as unlikely to catch up with their more evolved contemporaries. These views were mainstream views at the time. With this pseudo-evolutionary paradigm, it was assumed that Aboriginal Australians would die out once confronted with the "superior" Europeans. The mechanisms, to be sure, were glossed over. As a sop to Western science, Europeans thought that Aboriginal Australians should be studied. Scientists were intensely interested in the Aborigines' perceived lack of intelligence, and they felt the need to study them as genetic and cultural forebears of the superior Europeans. Again the Europeans were seeking to self-justify their prejudices and the conquest of Australia. Differing skull capacity and other anthropological data were put forward as evidence of and justification for the dominance of the European peoples. Ironically slavery, mainly of African origin Black people, was abolished in the British Empire in 1807, although it persisted in England itself until a new Emancipation Act in 1833. Slavery did continue in some British colonies for another century. In Australia convicts, Aborigines and later "Kanakas", indentured labourers, South Sea Islanders, filled the role vacated by the slaves. Until recently, these groups were not considered worthy of mention in official and school textbook versions of history.

John Locke (1689) added intellectual weight to this argument by theorising that labour added to land equalled property. When it came to Aboriginal lands in the Australian colonies, the Europeans, like John McDouall Stuart traversing Central Australia, the land of the Arabana, could not see the work of Aboriginal people in making the land like a great park. They discounted their efforts, which have now been written about by Bruce Pascoe in *Dark Emu* and Bill Gammage in *The Biggest Estate on Earth*. As with all Aboriginal Australians, the Arabana moulded nature for productive purposes for thousands of years, but this work, this labour, was invisible to European eyes.

From a religious perspective, Europeans believed that the truths of Christianity had to be shared with and taken as their own by ignorant or inferior peoples not yet acquainted with this religion.

Missionaries and similar workers were among the early arrivals in the Australian Europeans' influx. Ministers of religion had been influential in the movement to abolish slavery, asserting the common humanity of slaves and free, but these views clearly had their limits in the periphery of the British Empire. Arabana were latecomers to this formal religious intervention. The United Aborigines Mission (UAM) at Oodnadatta did not open until 1924, some sixty years after white settlement of the area, and after the post World-War 1 pandemic of influenza had killed nearly half of the Arabana population. The Mission at Finniss Springs followed even after this in 1939. Actually and paradoxically, rather than training for subservience, this latter Mission school helped Francis Dunbar Warren, the landholder, and the Arabana and other Aboriginal children to prepare for their entry into the wider world of the settler society and economy and for higher grade work on the Ghan.

Agriculturally the settler colonists sought to create "neo-Europes", importing and growing plants and raising beasts from the old Europe, to then send "home" and feed the population of the metropole, pandering to their dietary tastes. Native plants and animals were either overlooked or dismissed as pests taking feed from the desired European ones. That Aborigines thrived on the native plants and animals was ignored. After the colonial depopulation of the Aboriginal Australian population of the continent, there arose an erroneous idea that the so-called 'natives' were few because of the poor native food stocks. Arabana had to re-orient their food acquisition practices to what the pastoralists could and would provide, what ration stations issued and some residual hunting and gathering. Given this situation, the Ghan in this situation became a lifeline for food and other necessary supplies.

In South Australia, the South Australia Act, or Foundation Act of

1834 stated clearly that the British Crown regarded South Australia as "waste and unoccupied lands". The British population had burgeoned in the eighteenth and nineteenth centuries. This was seen as a natural reason to (a) feed them from colonial lands' produce and (b) export many people to make the world as British as possible. As many as one in six people from England emigrated in the nineteenth century. One key role of the railways was to supply the centre of the Empire, England, with foodstuffs, sheep and cattle products, as well as raw materials such as wool and minerals. In Arabana land the main export even nowadays is cattle by road trains to seaports and Australian cities.

Another theorist, Wolfe, added to these ideas of "natural racial superiority" with the paradoxical one of the "logic of elimination". This theory states that the settler colonists wanted nothing but the land, so Aboriginal peoples were extraneous and to be replaced like the native fauna and flora with European stock. Indeed Aboriginal Australians were sometimes counted with the native flora and fauna, indicative of their social standing in relation to settler society and perceived subhuman status. But when this replacement failed to occur or where there was labour shortfall, Aborigines became a variable workforce, to be used where labour was scarce or when times were good and required more workers, but to be turned off when times were bad or where European labour was available. Missionaries were party to this devil's bargain in some ways when they formed reservoirs of labour called "missions".

Similarly, Jean-Paul Sartre suggested that there is a contradiction inherent in the colonial system. He stated "the system wills simultaneously the death and multiplication of its victims". This is because a large labour force of the Indigenous keeps labour costs low, whereas their elimination or assimilation would cause costs to rise. Arabana have been at times in low numbers, for instance after epidemics, and sometimes quite populous, whereupon other means of oppression such as child removal and incarceration were put in place. The Ghan railway removed them from this "boom and bust" cycle by offering ongoing opportunities.

Labour Relations

Work is conceived of in a variety of ways by different theorists. Feudal times were associated with the idea of a master who owned the bodies and labour of peasants. It took the Black Death and the breakdown of readily available labour in Europe, and numerous other variables such as the growth of the idea of individualism in the Enlightenment, for this to be gradually replaced by the idea of workers as vendors of skills and labour to bosses and managers. Australian Aborigines, however, partly because of the race theory were seen as outside this system and treated more like slaves or beasts of burden than fellow humans and workers. It is a fact that Arabana and other Aboriginal workers were often in receipt of no pay, were not able to leave their employment on threat of punishment up to death, were given rations and clothing only, and were not even considered to own the work tools they used.

The case of the Arabana, however, differed from many other Aboriginal people. The railway ran through their land. Opportunity rather than solely threat stemmed from the iron horse. As Arabana Elder Reg Dodd said: "The railways were good to us". C.D. Rowley, writing in *The Remote Aborigines* in 1970, had seen that Australian colonialism as particularly destructive to the pre-invasion peoples' cultures: "(they) took all the land and only the land – ie, on which even the labour of the Aboriginal was unwanted as long as other labour was available". But Rowley was taken aback by Marree in Arabana country which was scrutinised in 1965, stating:

"There was apparently little difference in employment or other status between Aboriginal and other, although the reserve group would probably depend either on pensions or on the pastoral wages paid to Aborigines. ...the main wage employment was on the railway, which is the type of employment in which from one end of Australia to the other the Aboriginal worker seems most welcome...There is another side to all this, and it indicates a quiet assumption of responsibility on the part of Aboriginal people" (Rowley, op cit, p76).

Rowley's position was contradicted by the folklorist and populist historian, Patsy Adam-Smith, in her 1971 work *Romance of Australian Railways*, which shows how the facts were obscured even by respected writers. Adam-Smith collected 'campfire' stories from railway workers, but the Aboriginal Australians rarely featured. In fact, she says forthrightly, "Aborigines have never cared for railway work". Adam-Smith's work slotted into the old accepted false idea on Aboriginal Australians; they were not prepared to work. It also pre-dated academic inquiry in to the contributions of Aboriginal workers to the settler economy. Adam-Smith's comments could go unchallenged because there was a limited scholarship about this when she wrote it in the 1970s.

The formal literature on Aboriginal labour is a slowly emerging field. Ann McGrath and Kay Saunders collection from the 1990s commented on the limited material despite the obvious use of Aboriginal Australians in the Australian and colonial workforces from the outset of settlement. Ann Curthoys and Clive Moore in 1995 also surveyed the then extant information, emphasising that it was "abundantly clear" that historians had ignored the presence of Aboriginal workers over the two centuries of permanent white presence. Curthoys and Moore's collection rarely mentions Indigenous railway workers except for a brief mention by the former of Torres

Strait Islanders on page 15.

In more recent reviews of labour history for Aboriginal people, the Aboriginal contribution to the railways has still been neglected, though Keen in 2010 also notes the involvement of Torres Strait Islanders. Most recently, however, the researcher Katie Maher writing in 2014, discovered that lots of Aboriginal people had worked on the construction of railway lines in NSW, Queensland, South Australia, Western Australia and the Northern Territory as packers and carriers, sleeper cutters and track layers. Women also worked as laundresses and washerwomen. This book draws on some of the available information in the later chapter called "Aboriginal Australians in the Railways".

With the arrival of settlers, it has been suggested, many women found the pastoralists, police, "Afghan" cameleers and train construction workers, including Indians, Chinese and white people, offered a better life for them. These women left traditional Aboriginal male authority and labour structures behind. Whatever the reasons, the children of such connections form a large part of the population of Aboriginal Australians today, including the Arabana. The arrival of railways in 1884 in Arabana lands was not entirely a discontinuity with changes already happening but it greatly accelerated them. The concertinaing of distance, great numbers of new people, both Aboriginal and non-Aboriginal, and a large number of new available roles once the railway arrived all constituted a significant shift allowing Arabana access to the settler economy.

Work on railways is diverse: coal shoveller, train driver, fireman, carriage attendant, cleaner, caterer, toilet worker, porter, fettler, ganger, train examiner, engineer, train repair and maintenance worker, ticket seller, station hand and so on. Virtually all these roles were occupied by Arabana workers from the late 1920s onwards once the

Commonwealth Railways assumed control. I attach an extract from the Railway Commissioner's Report for 1930 which indicates the broad range of required recruits, into some of which roles Arabana stepped. In the chapter entitled "Arabana Working on the Railway" I cover the roles which named Arabana undertook.

Training for these jobs and trades can involve an array of subsidiary skills such as being able to read and write, understand diagrams and technical drawings, and to use the language of the settlers in professional ways. Initially, however, work obtained was through "walk-up" hiring usually for a day or a few days. No extensive human resource management involvement - just show up and talk to the ganger. As recorded in the conversations under "Arabana Family Stories", Arabana seized these opportunities from the outset where allowed. Much later, education and formal processes supervened. The first Arabana train driver, John Hodgson, qualified in 1968. Reg Dodd, train examiner from 1966 to 1986, is Arabana, as is Mervyn Dodd who became the yardmaster at Port Augusta. There has been negligible writing about such Aboriginal participation.

Human Transport in South Australia

Prior to trains being invented and used from 1826 onwards, the main means of transport for humans and their goods in South Australia was horses or camels, or wagons drawn by these animals. Although river transport was used in the eastern States, this was not possible in South Australia. Away from the Murray-Darling system, the rivers were few and sporadic in flow. The steam engine changed transport and rail transport virtually immediately became a substantial part of the way of life for a whole century from the 1820s on worldwide and in South Australia from the 1850s.

A railway is a revolutionary technology in the following ways: it shrinks distances twenty to thirty-fold because of the speed of the train. A journey formerly taking many weeks can be accomplished in a day. Trains carry vast quantities of goods – for export, for import - and can be used for altering or adjusting earlier modes of customary activities. In the Arabana's case it initially enabled 20-30Kg lumps of Pukardu, Arkapa, sacred red ochre, to be carried back to their country's sacred sites, as far as 300Km away, in a day rather than three weeks. With settler society, sheep or cattle raised in the Arabana lands were able to be transported for export to Adelaide in three days rather than weeks with smaller losses en route. People themselves travel upon trains for many purposes: business, trade, curiosity, flight from pursuers or persecutors, as stolen individuals, to move to far places to better their lot, even to gamble, commit crimes, and all these activities can occur in large amounts and numbers.

On a more sombre note, this book also notes that "trouble spots" can be controlled using the railways. "Well done steam! Smoke, thou art wonderful, and a reformer! "enthused the English General Sir Charles Napier, writing in 1839, who was thrilled to be able to travel by train to London, ready to load troops to quash a threatened rebellion in Manchester, England. Troops can be sent by train in record time, as occurred in the American Civil War from 1861 to 1865 and in the Canadian war against the rebellious Metis in 1885. The sudden

> ...permanent office, it is desired to advise that since the last certificate was given in terms of Section 50 there has been considerable expansion in Commonwealth Railways operations owing to the extension of the Central Australia Railway from Oodnadatta to Alice Springs, and the extension of the Trans-Australian Railway from Port Augusta to Port Pirie Junction.
>
> These extensions, together with the fast Trans-Australian Railway express service, have required the employment of additional regular employees, and, in terms of Section 50 of the Act, the Commissioner desires to submit to the Honorable the Minister his certificate that the following wages employees are now necessary for the working and maintenance of the Trans-Australian and Central Australia Railways:—
>
> | Group | Number |
> |---|---|
> | Chargeman, Cleaner, Chef, Checker, Conductor, Engine-Driver, Fireman, Fuelman, Guard, Assistant Guard, Kitchenman, Motor Driver, Motor Lorry Driver, Packer and Trimmer, Pantryman, Porter, Pumper, Shunter, Train Examiner, Waiter, Washer-out, Wharf Foreman, and Youth | 337 |
> | Apprentice, Blacksmith, Boilermaker, Carbuilder, Carpenter, Car-Trimmer, Coppersmith, District Lineman, Driller, Electrician, Fitter, Fitter-in Charge, Foreman, Machinist, Mason, Motor Mechanic, Moulder, Painter, Patternmaker, Plumber, Turner, Welder, and other artisans, Crane Driver, Electric Crane Driver, Canvas Worker, Train Lighting Examiner, Foundry Furnaceman, Helper, Horse Driver, Laborer, Lifter, Metaller, Slinger, Storeman, Spray Painter, Stationary Engine-Driver, Striker, Watchman, and Wireman | 383 |
> | Ganger and Fettler, Cook (Maintenance Gang) | 539 |

Staff numbers for Commonwealth Railways 1930

arrival of extra police or troops was a possibility in Arabana country, although never required.

Even in a very recent history from 2010, the author, Robert Lee, writes of Aborigines and transport as if the local peoples were and are uninvolved in anything other than pre-colonial modes of transport, let alone working upon the railways from early times. This book shows that this is not true. And a popular recent book by ABC journalist Paul Lockyer from 2011 (who unfortunately died at Lake Eyre) only has Arabana mentioned in his Chapter 1, not contemporaneously. Even Stephen Brooke's recent old-fashioned titled book *Australian Railways: How the Land Was Conquered* comes from the same year, 2011!

Transport: "Corridor Theory"

A theorist, C. Whebell, has put forward a theory of "corridors", initially in urban systems. His initial idea proposed five stages in a developing economic landscape: initial occupance (in Australia's case, overwriting former occupation), commercial agriculture, railway transport, motor transport (not invented of course in 1884) and metropolitanism. Others have expanded this theoretical perspective. In South Australia this assumed fivefold sequence has not occurred, as the commercial agriculture has always been fragile and urbanisation of "remote" towns like Marree and Oodnadatta has not occurred. Nonetheless the idea of a corridor is useful. "A corridor does not just join formerly discrete places. It is its own type of place" writes Alan Mayne. Railways may threaten previously held notions of place, as indeed they did and do with Arabana, but simultaneously they set up different connections and perspectives. There is a poetics of corridors, as Bachelard wrote, because it pays attention at the same time to the "impersonal and the intimate, the public and the private, the mobile and the static". The railway corridor consists of diverse places, some permanent and some transient, within which people live and work. In Arabana country this meant that the old Dreaming Tracks, Songlines, pilgrimage and trade routes were partially overwritten by a new settler-colonist narrative, that of white ownership of territory, agriculture, and a relationship to a remote metropole.

The philosopher Heidegger would characterise this as "gathering" landscapes and cultures, which "generates new places, perspectives, meanings and experiences". The railway has been instrumental in shaping a multicultural postcolonial federalism. The Ghan reformed the identities of the regions through which it passed and the people within that corridor. Inside the train itself, the compartment creates new places for negotiations around meanings and experiences. Watching the landscape flash past is an entirely different perspective from walking it. The usually transient relationships between passengers are utterly different from those of the workers watching the train go by. Arabana were initially beside but then quickly on the train also. Their identities, already changing, transformed from tribal estate, country-based to that also associated with the corridor and its characteristics.

One striking comment from explorer John McDouall Stuart was his enthusiastic description of Arabana country as "wonderful country, scarcely to be believed" (Sunday 5th June 1859 near Mt Younghusband). He noted "native tracks" everywhere and met people not infrequently. But what does he mean by this "wonderful country"? Fit for sheep or cattle to graze upon. He thinks of the manicured grass plains as ripe for European animals and not as the source of seed for feeding all these "natives" he has seen. And proto-agriculture, as Bruce Pascoe in *Dark Emu* has written about, is beyond his ken. McDouall Stuart was not averse to the new railway technology: for his fifth expedition in 1861 he travelled on the train to Kapunda, then the terminus, which is only 80Km north of Adelaide, before taking to his horse.

Surveying for the train line in Arabana country was carried out partly by George Warren, uncle of Francis Dunbar Warren, pastoralist and descendant of the first John Warren of Springfield and Strangways Station. Strangways was the first Station established in Arabana country, in 1863. Francis's Uncle George Warren (21/9/1820 - 26/2/1895), had involvement from Arabana men of the Strangways Station who helped survey for the train line between Marree and further west and north. John Ross, another surveyor, also had major assistance from the Macumba Arabana Aborigines.

This book expands the information about a resilient people who have endured the time of invasion and its aftermath of continued colonial impact. It links the domains of Aboriginal, labour and transport history in detailing how the Arabana negotiated the incursion of white settler society on their country. It expands on the work of previous writers who have explored the contributions of Indigenous labour to Australia's development. As will be revealed in this book, the Arabana were crucial contributors in one of Australia's most important infrastructure projects, the Old Ghan railway. By drawing on their stories, this book starts to fill an important gap, by showing how Aboriginal Australians were and are important contributors in the development of Australia's infrastructure.

*Strangways Springs Station Panoramic view looking south west.
(Photograph Courtesy of the State Library of South Australia [B 1486])*

Strangways Springs Station: Kitchen and men's hut from the South East (Photograph Courtesy of the State Library of South Australia [B 1487])

2

LIVING IN THE DESERT: AUSTRALIA'S RED HEART

The Arabana Before British Settlement

One of about two hundred and fifty distinct Indigenous peoples, the Arabana lived and flourished in some of the least hospitable (particularly to white people) country on the west of Lake Eyre, reclaimed name as *Kati Thanda* since 2013, in the centre of the Australian continent. Lake Eyre was so named by Europeans after explorer John Eyre after a suggestion in the Adelaide *Register* of 27th January 1860. Most years this Lake is a dry salt pan. At about ten to fifteen year intervals the Lake floods, with the sources of water mostly far away in the Queensland coastal ranges. According to John Mulvaney and Johan Kamminga, writing in 1999, Indigenous people have inhabited the Lake and its surrounds for over 20,000 years although there was probably a temporary retreat during the severe glaciation period, the last glacial maximum. The Arabana called their country *Wangyu* or *Wadhlu* and Lake Eyre, *Bundu*, or *Kati Thanda*. One Aboriginal Australian story given about the Lake's origin is that of a kangaroo skin, thrown down by an ancestor, which then filled with water.

The pre-colonial lifestyle of the Arabana consisted of observing the Law/Lore/*Ularaka*. This lore is transmitted by stories, called

Wibma, which are tales with mnemonic, moral, mythic and legal aspects and usually associated with particular locations and ceremonies of maintenance or increase. Their land is a "storied landscape". These stories both name and bring spiritual significance to the land, and reflect that there was, and still is, an Arabana way of interpreting the country. For instance, one Dreaming Track to do with two dingos followed mound springs down from between Coober Pedy and William Creek (*Cadiwarrawirracanna* {shortened name}– stars dancing on water) to the ochre (*arrkapa*) mines near Parachilna.

Another important Dreaming Track runs all the way from the Tiwi Islands through Arabana country down to Port Augusta. This is the *Urumbula*, or Native Cat (Quoll) Dreaming. One would expect that in many cultures such usurpation of critical resources like the sacred mound springs would have led to massive confrontation and loss of life by warfare or its frontier equivalent. It appears that in the case of the Arabana this did not occur.

In the way of life for Arabana in pre-colonial times, goods were not accumulated nor amassed for their own sake. Trade did occur for needed items not present in their own country from as far away as Cloncurry, but this was an equitable barter system and no excess value was retained. Marree was a terminus or trade entrepôt where pituri from the northeast, stone mortars and pestles, spear shafts, furs, seeds and ochre were all traded. In addition, the Arabana were reputed to be specialists in making netted bags for trade. As they lacked stone for axe heads in their country, they traded for these from the Macdonnell Ranges and Queensland. On the other hand, they had stone for mortars and traded these into Simpson Desert areas.

There was no exploitation of land to exhaustion nor of labour, and there was no division between a working life and any other aspect of existence. Want did occur in poor seasons such as droughts or extensive flooding and this could lead to visitation to neighbours temporarily. When white settler society entered Arabana country, it was engaging with a people with long established trade ties to other Indigenous groups. The white settlers and workers became another group through which the Arabana could extend these ties.

Agriculture in Arabana country predating European settlement is known to have occurred. Mitchell Grass (Astrebela pectinata) and Native Millet (*Panara* or *Panera*, Panicum decompositum) known as *Nardoo* grow in Arabana country and it is known that this was harvested, the seeds ground and bread made. This crop was planted deliberately. The train station name Wangianna means "winnowing dish" in Arabana language, indicating the prevalence of this activity nearby. (This is very ironic when the white people renamed Government Gums, further down the railway line, "Farina", Latin for wheat/flour which they erroneously hoped would grow there).

Yams (including *Inka*,{Vigna lanceolata} *Amapina* {large yam} and *ariltyi* {pencil yam}, *mutyarri*, *waRala*, and *yarra-karla* in Arabana are also mentioned by Freddie Ah Chee in Bruce Shaw's 1995 book, *Our Heart is The Land*. Algebuckina, a significant place on the Ghan line, actually means "digging yams". Other plants likely to be cultivated were button grass (Dactyloctenium radulans), Common purslane (Portulaca oleracea) and Bush tomato (Solanum ellipticum). "Bush onion" (*Yalka* in Arabana; Cyperus bulbosus) used to grow near Curdimurka and Coward Springs and many other parts of Arabana country as well. Such onions could grow to about 30cm in diameter.

Indeed anthropologist Baldwin Spencer mentioned this onion plant as a significant food source when he was camped at Charlotte

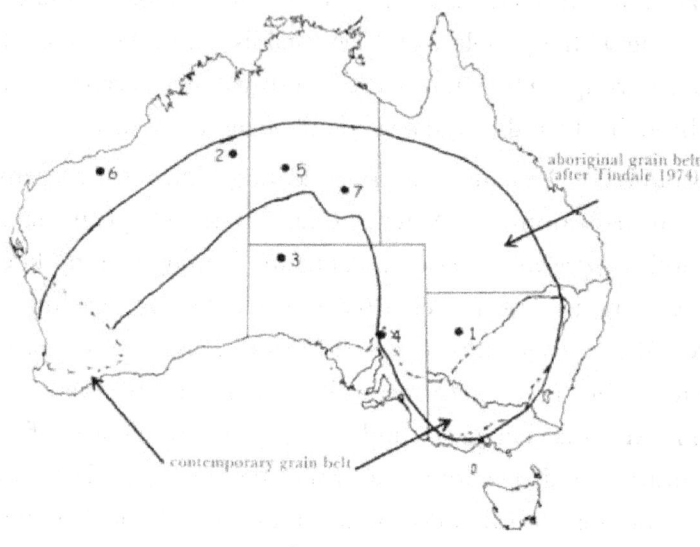

Aboriginal grain belt

(in Dark Emu, Pascoe, 2014, p 29, with permission)

at the north end of Arabana country. Poultry raising was also an intermittent activity. When *Kati Thanda*/Lake Eyre had water in it, pelicans nested there and had chicks. These chicks were corralled and then eaten like chickens today in western diet. The convenience was that the parents kept feeding the chicks instead of Arabana having to do it.

In the Marree Arabunna (sic) Community Centre, there are several types of fighting boomerangs and shields. This implies that interpersonal conflicts and community versus community conflicts did occur between males, although the scale must have been small. In Aboriginal communities, women also fought, using their digging sticks, various clubs and opportunistic stones. Revenge parties also travelled to neighbouring tribes to wreak vengeance on a perceived malefactor, who may have been identified as causing an unnatural death among Arabana. Such scraps or "tribal" feuding were largely disregarded by white people once they arrived, even if fatalities occurred.

Bundu or Kati Thanda

Lake Eyre, called, inter alia, *Bundu* (salt lake) and reclaimed by the name of *Kati Thanda* (no known translation) by the Arabana in 2013, was "discovered" by Europeans in 1839. Major flooding occurred in 2010 for the first time in over a decade. Great Artesian Basin freshwater springs do break though and one, Dingo Island in the middle of the Lake, is used by dingoes to give birth to and rear their young. Other creation stories around Finniss Springs Station towards the southern end of Arabana country (named after Boyle Travers Finniss, first Premier of South Australia in 1856) concern the various natural features and include: Pregnant Woman (*Bullaburra*), Crested Pigeon (*Mulapara*), Three Brothers, and Bearded Dragon (*Kudni*).

Red Ochre and Pituri Before the Railway

Aboriginal men made pilgrimage trips to a Red Ochre mine in the Flinders Ranges along Dreaming tracks established probably for thousands of years. Before the railway and other modes of transport, the returning men would carry a 30-35Kg moulded lump of Red Ochre on their heads. When the camels and their cameleers arrived in

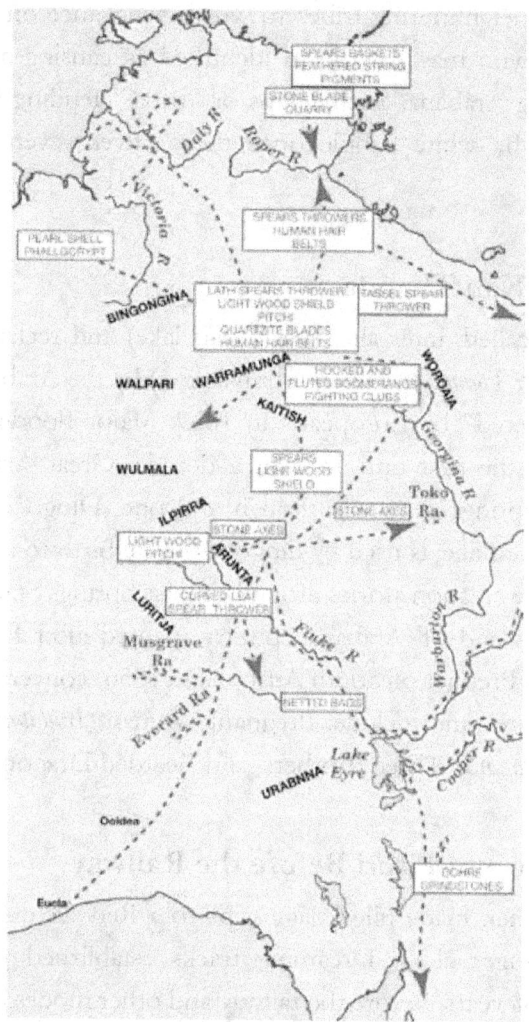

Aboriginal trade routes

(Kerwin, 2010, with permission)

their country, Arabana and other tribes commissioned the cameleers to carry their loads instead, while they still walked back to their traditional lands. Later, loads of red ochre and pituri were also carried by mail coach (Jones, op cit, p372).

Arrival of Explorers and the Coming of White Settlers

By the 1850s there were probably about 800-1,000 Arabana, living in small groups scattered across the landscape, with concentrations near the sacred mound springs and near other permanent water holes. Europeans did not penetrate this area until the 1830s, fifty years after the Port Jackson Sydney colony, and not in any significant numbers.

John McDouall Stuart, exploring the area in 1858 and 1859, however, did not echo the idea of a "dead heart" or "red centre". He used expressions such as "...the range is a beautiful grass country to the very top. In the creeks the grass and other plants are growing luxuriantly..." around Finniss Springs, "good feeding country, timbered with box and gum-trees", "we came to the banks of the two creeks passed by Major Warburton, splendidly grassed", and near Chambers Creek "About four miles from last night's camp the chain of large water holes commences, and continues beyond to-night's camp. They are indeed most splendid water holes — not holes, but very long ponds; they are nearly one continuous sheet of water, and the scenery is beautiful". Again he journaled on 9th May 1859 "I have not seen better runs in the colony, and in the driest summer the furthest distance from water will not be above five miles at the most, but the feed is so abundant that they would not require to go so far". Gammage, as noted above, emphasises that there was blindness to the managed estate aspect of these terrains and the estate managers, the Arabana. Otherwise the local people would have to have been regarded as "gentry", proper landholders, and a usurper could not do that. When white settlers arrived, the whole Arabana population was dispossessed, under the continued fiction of *Terra Nullius*, the country mostly re-named, and they were denied political, economic, social and human rights despite notionally being British subjects.

Smallpox

It would appear that a smallpox epidemic swept through the Arabana in 1858 or 1859, just five years before Strangways Station, the first pastoral station, was established. This epidemic probably caused the death of about fifty per cent of the Arabana population according to Dick Kimber writing in 1988. Because of the epidemic's toll, it seems possible that Arabana society was disorganized by this "invisible invader", and the society was thus less able to mount any strong armed resistance to the pastoralists, as had happened elsewhere.

Pastoral Leases And The Overland Telegraph Line
European Settlement of South Australia

In May 1839, William Wyatt, the then "Protector of Aborigines", announced publicly that it appeared that the natives occupied no lands in the especial manner described in the original instructions. Indeed, the settlers passed separate legislation to justify their activities. There was an earlier Aborigines Ordinance Act, No. 12 of 1844 on the books, but when the colony become self-governing in 1857, the statute virtually became a dead letter. The official duties of the Chief Protector and Sub-Protectors were as follows: "watch over the general interests of the Aborigines, and be the responsible means of communication with the Government"; "dispense justice summarily, in all matters of dispute between natives themselves, as also between natives and Europeans, to the extent of at one inflicting punishment on the native, if the culpable party, or of committing the

European for trial, if it was evident that he had infringed the law in a gross manner". The Chief Protector was supposed to be assisted by the Sub-Protectors to attend to the physical needs especially of the aged, infirm and ill, to train Aboriginal people "to steady industrial habits and manners of civilised life" and to open their minds to "the truths of Christianity". There was, however, no Chief Aboriginal Protector appointed from 1856 onwards until new 1911 legislation, over fifty years later. The functions of the Chief Protector were to be overseen by the Commissioner for Public Works; there was no separate department. In fact settlers and police in the far north of South Australia were left pretty much to their own devices regarding their treatment of Aborigines by the Government for that whole fifty year period.

There were Sub-Protectors such as the minister John Parker Buttfield {1822-1885} (appointed 1866 and lived at Blinman; also Special and Stipendary Magistrate from 1869) over that time but most tended to be Police Officers such as Inspector Bryan Besley based as far south as Port Augusta, in post from 1892 to 1900. The reports from these men show the tenor of the Protection. Control and perhaps education was the *leitmotif*. Only Buttfield was in post prior to the Great Northern Railway being laid as far as Arabana country. The treatment of Aborigines in the north could be benign or malign. In his seminal *The Destruction of Aboriginal Society*, Rowley states "... race relations were a matter for the settler and the local Aborigines without effective Government interference" (Rowley, 1970, p 205). This is a possibly unique situation in Australia where every other Government imposed increasingly severe restrictions on native peoples from as early as possible. But "South Australia beyond the farming areas... formed another whole region where the settlers were subject mainly to their own consciences for many decades" (Rowley, op cit, p 206).

Some sub-protectors were diligent in their duties, and their reports detail the plights of the Indigenous peoples in the north. An example from 1867, four years after Strangways Station was established, is as follows: "There has been a great amount of sickness but little mortality among the natives. ... I always carry in my waggonette medicine and medical comforts and thus have been enabled to render needful assistance to many poor sufferers....The almost total absence of native animals, and the failure of other resources (*this was in the middle of a severe drought*), have placed a large number of Aborigines in most trying circumstances and dependant upon the government's generosity....They are for the most part patient, peaceable and well disposed, occasionally an unprotected hut is robbed of stores and there have been one or two instances of crimes of a more aggravated nature". No further comments nor investigations apparently ensued about these "crimes of a more aggravated nature". In 1868 Buttfield wrote "I can note no appreciable increase of native animals. For years to come the Aborigines will remain more or less dependant upon the government for support, a contingency which would not have arisen but for the flocks and herds of the invader during the long and disastrous drought". Some years later, however, he reported that the Aborigines had endured great hardships and many had died from sheer want. Buttfield's reports highlight that the introduction of the sheep and cattle industry had led to a decrease in the traditional Indigenous food sources. A major cause of this was the establishment of Strangways Springs Station in 1863.

Strangways

Although now abandoned, Strangways Springs Station was the first pastoral property in the west of Lake Eyre area in the traditional land of the Arabana. This region had been explored by both McDouall

Stuart and Peter Warburton in the previous five years. It was set up by Julius Jeffreys, future member of Parliament, John Warren, one of the founder members of the Pastoralists' Union in 1890, and William Bakewell, who served as Crown Solicitor. The local Arabana both male and female were enlisted as free or cheap labour to care for the sheep.

The administration of Strangways in the early 1860s was disturbed by increasingly large Aboriginal parties travelling through on the red ochre dreaming track on the western side of the Flinders Ranges. These parties increased in size in the 1860s, partly because of the numbers of sheep and cattle available as food sources. The climate was also quite favourable before a drought from 1864-5. It would also appear that Aboriginal groups had also started coming for plunder from the settlers.

Julius Jeffreys called for police protection in 1863, the same year he and his colleagues had set up Strangways. So first appropriation of the land occurred then a call for "legitimate" police protection from the real local people. He wrote in June 1863 "it is with much regret that I have the honour to inform you that the Aborigines have now become really dangerous and unless immediate steps are taken by the government some frightful calamity will take place" (South Australian Parliamentary Papers 1863). Just five months later, in November 1863, a massacre did occur at Beltana, south of Arabana country, to a red ochre pilgrimage party. Probably fifty Aboriginal men were killed or died of wounds. Even prior to that, Police Commissioner Peter Warburton had toured the area. He wrote to the Government "I do not deny that the settlers at times suffer loss from the natives, but I do not think the only remedy lies in shooting the plunderers" (South Australian Parliamentary Papers 1864, No. 134, tabled 20th October 1863). He recommended that the red ochre pilgrimage parties be offered rations at the main homesteads of each station to avoid conflict as they passed through. This ground breaking relatively benign policy was implemented slowly. There had been ration stations from the late 1830s-1840s but they proliferated after Warburton's recommendation.

At Strangways in 1865, the manager John Churchill Oastler originally resisted Warburton's benign idea, and dealt with a passing party by putting a bullet into a stump near the demanding Aborigines, who sensibly fled. Interestingly the demand had been put in pidgin English, which the spokesman had already learned. In drought years, ochre parties dwindled.

The whole Arabana area was subject to drought in the late 1860s and Strangways lost 6,500 sheep. A mortgage was taken out with Thomas Hogarth, John Warren's father-in-law, and the station managed to struggle on. About 150 Arabana were living at Strangways by then. Some continued to live traditionally but there was regular interchange between the groups. Roles for both male and female Arabana at Strangways included being shepherds, lambing surveillance, shearing and wool scouring, dogging, tracking and fence repair. In earlier days, Arabana also showed white people areas to graze and water the stock. Some work was seasonal and some fulltime. Only a very few Arabana received any pay. Most were given rations and minimal clothing.

Over the 1870s and 1880s, the two groups, Aborigines and settlers, gradually came to an accommodation along the lines suggested by Warburton. Strangways acted as a ration station as did its replacement Anna Creek, later on. Later there were government sponsored ration stations rather than just private ones. There were Arabana encampments near the railway after the Oodnadatta extension opened in 1891 at Bangadillina Creek near Warrina, Duff Creek, Oodloodlana Spring, Algebuckina and some other places along the line such as

Curdimurka. Strangways Springs Station continued to be operated as a sheep station until about 1900 when operations were transferred to Anna Creek. Strangways continued as a repeater station for the Overland Telegraph. In 1875, just twelve years after the arrival of British settler-colonists at Strangways Springs Station, Frank J. Gillen wrote that "all the shepherds employed at this station are Niggers [sic] ...and do just as well as the whites".

Sheep Station Settlement Patterns

In addition to the head station with stone buildings and permanent facilities, early sheep stations (ca 1860-1882) included residential outstations, where in seasons with adequate rainfall, large numbers of sheep could be kept on rainwater; smaller outstations near permanent springs where uncertain rain conditions required smaller groups of sheep; and work camps, for scouring and shearing sheep. Later adaptations included new technologies, such as bores dug into artesian deposits for permanent access to water and the addition of railroad spurs.

Apart from relationships, trade and artefacts, Professor Alistair Paterson has written of the environmental degradation of the Strangways Spring area, brought about by the introduction of these new animal species, the construction of fencing, and the over-use and mismanagement of artesian water resources. Most importantly, Paterson traced the complex changes in the pattern of interaction between Aboriginal and European populations. In all, he concluded, the complexity revealed in the documents and archaeological studies suggest a two-way process of adaptation and change, as the technology changed, and as the two groups learned to adapt to one another.

Strangways Station partially relocated north to Anna Creek Station in 1872. John Hogarth ran Anna Creek until 1893, followed by his younger brother Thomas until 1913. George Warren followed for twelve months, then Francis, his younger brother until 1918. The Station was sold in 1918 to Malcolm Reid and Leslie Taylor. Malcolm Reid was a brother of Sidney Reid, who was married to Elma, a daughter of Sir Sidney Kidman. Kidman had 33% of the property by 1927 and owned it all by 1934.

Edward Cranswick, whom I met with Kevin Buzzacott, Arabana elder, in 2012, has written of Anna Creek. He says (https://candobetter.net/ node/436) "My grandfather's family were members of the Hogarth-Warren business partnership that began with the marriage of his aunt, Margaret Hogarth, to John Warren in 1865, and it became one of the largest pastoralist enterprises in South Australia in the late 1800's -- Anna Creek, SA, now the world's largest working cattle station, occupying an area greater than that of Israel, was just one of their properties". He is certain that "The success of the family business was based on the presence and labour of hundreds of Aboriginal people, mostly Arabuna [sic], who worked on the station, starting with the many Aboriginal stockmen who mustered the thousands of cattle and sheep; reciprocally, the Aboriginal people became dependent upon the rations provided by the pastoralists of European descent because the overgrazed land could no longer sustain the native food supply". This mixing of fortunes of the two peoples "inevitably" led to "the mixing of blood", that is marriage and the like, and the production of "mixed race" children. He adds "I have met many of my cousins of Aboriginal descent whose grandfather was Francis Dunbar Warren, a pastoralist who had married the Arabuna [sic] mother of his children as formally as was then possible for a black and white to marry in that day.

Francis acted to live the best life with those with whom he shared life -- their example is a light from the past that beckons us into the future".

These relationships assisted the Arabana people to enter the dominant settler society and economy. Indeed, by the turn of the nineteenth century the Arabana were pivotal to the Warren-Hogarth pastoral empire. Other developments in the region would reinforce their importance to the settler economy.

The Overland Telegraph Line

The Overland Telegraph line was put through from 1870 - 1872 from Port Augusta on the Spencer Gulf to Darwin. In Arabana country, this line followed the mound springs shown to the explorers and surveyors by Arabana. John McDouall Stuart had returned to Arabana country in 1862 to survey for the Telegraph line. Pastoral settlement followed and Arabana were incorporated into this project, as noted above, but also utilised in subsequent surveying for the settlers and the telegraph, because Stuart's maps were fragmentary and eight years out of date. For instance, another surveyor, John Ross, "enterprising young manager of Thomas Elder's far north cattle stations" (Moyal, 1984, p43), appointed by Todd on 7th July 1870, was exploring hundreds of kilometres ahead of the construction crews. He evidently had Arabana companions or guides as he used the Arabana name for *Koorakarinna* waterhole on Frew's Creek. Alfred Giles was a member of this expedition and stated that Frew's Creek was properly called *Cookoolinah*. This is an Arabana word *kukurla* meaning plump little bandicoot. Ross could clearly communicate with Arabana people, most probably those who had been on Umbum Station south of Oodnadatta.

In John Ross's diary of that expedition, he also uses other Arabana names for geographic features: *Algebuckina* ("digging yams" in Arabana) waterhole and *Cadnia-Owie* Creek and waterhole.

Overland telegraph Line 1870-72 (reconstruction),
(personal collection)

The Aboriginal members of his expedition are quite "invisible" (even horses are named but not the Aboriginal people) and only mentioned in one place. On Sunday 15th January 1871, a white member of the expedition, Hearne, had been missing for several days. Ross writes "...sent Hearne 'a good tracker' (unnamed) mounted on the best and only shod horse I have got..." Other Overland Telegraph and Great Northern Railway surveyors' field notebooks (GRG35/258) do not contain such details. It is most likely that the Arabana came from Peake Station or, as noted, Umbum Station.

This very Aboriginal invisibility is exactly what this book seeks to dispel. Most expeditions had Aboriginal Australians accompanying them, even if not acknowledged. The later Ernest Giles expedition across Australia, for instance, had Tommy (Oldham) and the Aboriginal Australian accompanying Stuart on his first expedition has already been mentioned.

Marree - First Telegraph Station
(from Moyal, 1984, p21)

The settlement of Marree, at that time called Hergott Springs, became a large camp full of the builders of the telegraph line. A police presence in the form of three mounted constables only arrived in Hergott in 1882, some ten years after the Telegraph line was constructed, so the behaviour of the Telegraph line builders at that place may have been less troublesome than elsewhere. Charles Todd, instigator of the Telegraph, contributed to Curr's book, *The Australian Race: Its Origin, Languages, Customs, Place of Landing in Australia and The Routes By Which It Spread Itself Over the Continent*, with a hundred words of Arabana vocabulary (Curr, 1886, Chap 42, Vol 2, page 10-11).

There were eleven telegraph repeater stations set up along the line to boost the Morse code signal because it faded over distance. Two of these were on Arabana land. The repeater stations were located at Beltana, south of Arabana land, Strangways Springs and The Peake, both in Arabana country, then Charlotte Waters, more northern tribes, Alice Springs, Barrow Creek, Tennant Creek, Powell Creek,

Daly Waters and Yam Creek. Each repeater station was staffed by a stationmaster, with up to four operators and a linesman to repair line faults. As far as any documented records or oral history reports from Arabana to whom I spoke, Arabana did not become telegraph operators or any other position within these facilities.

By the 1880s, Arabana had been decimated by epidemics and their land taken from them. Despite this, depopulation by massacre and deliberate starvation, however, is not recorded for this area (Foster et al, 2001; Foster and Nettelbeck, 2012) although the Aboriginal Protector Buttfield reports talk of severe want in the 1860's drought seasons.

Travellers & Anthropologists and the Creation of Aboriginal Stereotypes

Accounts from anthropologists suffer from what has been described as a "fabled ethnographic present". By the time of anthropologists' recording Arabana lives and culture, the traditional practices had already altered as a result of the arrival of Europeans themselves. The anthropologists also seldom mention the real situation in which they found Arabana when they talked to them (through interpreters). Their impressions formed the basis for creating derogatory stereotypes about the Arabana. These stereotypes were disseminated in the colonies' major urban centres under the banner of scientific enquiry. The Arabana, being on the Telegraph and railway route, were prime candidates to be framed within this stereotype.

This is evident in the work of J. J. East who travelled through Arabana country in the mid-1880s. On 16 July 1886, J. J. East told the Field Naturalists' Section of the Royal Society about his trip through Arabana country. His views were subsequently published in his 1889 volume, *The Aborigines of Central and South Australia*. East noted, unflatteringly, that the "Urominna" were also called this by "neighbouring nations", meaning that they were a "literally short or small people". East noted that the "Urominna" were "physically the most unprepossessing natives of the province, and downright ugly in nature and disposition. Gratitude or kindness is totally unknown to them, and they are truculent to a degree. Furthermore, they believe that all deaths are due to "witchcraft." The "bewitcher" was thought to belong to a neighbouring tribe and had to be located and killed. The result was a series of raids between the Urominna and its nearest neighbouring tribe, the Kokatha. These raids were still happening in the 1920s and 1930s, and the remnants are evident in the Marree Arabunna (sic) Community Centre's collection of fighting boomerangs and shields which are on public display (personal observations, 2012, 3, 4). East, however, noted them and used them to assert his superiority over the Aboriginal Australians. East's most significant observation was that the Urominna were travellers, prepared to walk "long distances to the "Bookitta" ochre deposits near the Blinman, to obtain supplies of this pigment for ornamenting their persons." East was noting a journey that had already changed with the coming of the camelmen and the railway.

Moreover the anthropologists necessarily relied on limited numbers of informants. Baldwin Spencer and Frank Gillen travelled with two Aboriginal Australians – Erlikiliakirra and Purunda (aka Perrurle).

wick Perrurle and Jim Kite Erlikiyika
(Telegraph Station, Alice Springs)

Their expedition was utterly dependent on these guides who gave them entrée into Aboriginal communities. "Erlikiliakirra acted as a very important anthropological interpreter for them ... I've been through Spencer's notebook and it's quite clear that he just jotted down literally what he was being told and then he wrote it up for publication. So really it was Erlikiliakirra's material that provided a very large chunk of the book that Spencer and Gillen produced as a result of that expedition" (John Mulvaney on Radio National "100 Years, The Australian Story", 2001; Spencer, Walter Baldwin, 1928). Elkin (1931) in his article, 'The Social Organisation of South Australian Tribes", amended some ideas that Spencer and Gillen put in their book, mostly by having more informants, but did not fundamentally alter their findings. The focus of these anthropologists was to observe the Aborigines in what they perceived as their traditional state. In the case of the Arabana this could not be done. The Arabana had already been involved in the pastoral industry, mining, cameleering and the railway for twenty years by the time Spencer and Gillen made their records in 1899.

One interesting and possibly pertinent finding from both Spencer & Gillen (1899) and later the anthropologist Bronislaw Malinowski writing in 1913 was that when non-Aboriginal or even non-Arabana Aboriginal men arrived in Arabana country, one possible customary relationship which could be formed was called "Piraunguru". This was the giving of a married woman to an outsider without recriminations from the Arabana men, and indeed such relationships could be organised by a woman's elder brothers and the elders, so allowing for the dictum "where fraternity fails, maternity may prevail". Thus when male pastoralists, telegraph workers, miners, cameleers or railway workers entered into relationships with Arabana, they were considered by Arabana to have become honorary Arabana and their Piraunguru children were seen as Arabana.

This was highly adaptive of Arabana, as many of the incoming white workers were in the region only briefly, whereas the children stayed on with their mothers, being reared as Arabana and not taken away by the fathers, as would have happened in Victorian England at the time. The children staying in the Arabana meant learning that way of life, but ongoing contact with non-Arabana also meant that other learnings could occur. This is similar to what other writers call "hybridisation" "creolisation", "accommodation" or even "mimicry". But probably the best descriptor is "creation of fictive relationships", which is how McDonnell in 2015 describes a similar practice among the Great Lakes Indians of North America. Kinships are created which can lead to political influence and alliances. The Arabana had long used such relationships with Wangkanguru, Arrernte and Dieri in this regard although Kokatha seem to remain traditional rivals.

By way of a contrasting view, Mattingley and Hampton writing in 1988 suggest that Arabana women were taken by force by railway construction workers and other non-Aboriginal men, once they were in the country. Some assert that "rape and subjugation of Aboriginal women was a key feature in European/Aboriginal sexual relations". Mattingley and Hampton, however, do accept that some men formed permanent voluntary liaisons with Aboriginal women and this is what Arabana told me. And in any case, Piraunguru does not require permanence.

Indeed the best known Arabana woman was Topsy Smith, who founded The Bungalow in Alice Springs for Aboriginal children in 1914 with help from local policeman Sergeant Stott. Topsy was born about 1875, the daughter of Mary Kemp, an Arabana lady, and Arthur Evans, an Oodnadatta policeman, a white man. In her early teens Topsy was taken to see the new Railway, which was in fact, The Old Ghan. She married Bill Smith, a Welsh miner, another white man, in the early 1890s but he died about 1914 and Topsy took their large family to Alice Springs. Topsy and Ida Standley ran The Bungalow, a children's home, until the latter's retirement in 1929. As noted on the information boards of the National Pioneer Women's Hall of Fame, Topsy Smith died in Alice Springs on 15 April 1960. Smith was a strong woman, and throughout her long life there is no evidence of her been subjugated by, or subject to violence from, men. Smith was an example of the emerging Arabana who could not just survive in, but contribute to, the dominant white settler society. She was a product of a people who had learned to interact with, and adapt to the ways of the settlers. As is evident from the experiences of the Arabana and the pastoral workers of Strangways, Anna Creek and Finniss Springs' stations, they not only worked together, but also raised families in contravention of the laws of the day.

John Churchill Oastler, manager of Strangways and Anna Creek for many years in the later nineteenth century, had a very dark complexion. He wrote himself that he was held in high esteem by the local Arabana who saw him as the reincarnation of one of their famous chiefs, Makoonookoo Marunda (also quoted as Narcoo Noocamarunda) {Shaw, 1995, p 15). Oastler also says the Arabana called him "father". In any case, this cross-cultural identification as a reincarnation of a "chief" by both Oastler and the Arabana elders may have been a very clever way of binding and setting up relationships of mutual obligation. Oastler was a classical exemplar of the culture clash. He was utterly determined to "break these wild tribes into something like obedience, and to teach them that the law of ownership of property, and that their laws must give way to the white man's law" (Oastler, 1908, p205). But his published talk to Adelaide burghers may not be the entire truth. Did Oastler get given Aboriginal wives? This would be normal under the social structure of the Arabana. It is just possible that Oastler had Annie, his adopted son Kalli Kalli's sister, as a mate. Kalli Kalli is mentioned often in the correspondence and his sister, Annie, a "little shepherdess" also features. Oastler did marry a divorced white woman, Clarissa Sidney Pope on 23rd September 1884 at the age of 47 years, but they had no children.

In John Warren III's's memoirs (p7) he writes that his dad or uncles (William, Tom, Robert and David Hogarth) used to bring down herds of cattle for market with a popular Aboriginal stockman called Billy Rowdy (Ooloo dadloo Marunda) who, inter alia, used to entertain the three boys with his comedic impersonations. Paterson has photographs of Rowdy and his family on the cover of his book and in the text. This shows the closer personal but not necessarily sexual relationships with Arabana than many pastoral families.

During the 1860's, as noted above, drought ravaged many parts of

South Australia, and the Flinders Ranges did not escape these effects. Many of the Aboriginal people were forced to retreat from desert and turn to the ration depots set up by white people, where poor living conditions and disease wiped many more of the Aborigines out. By the mid 1870's many of the surviving Aborigines were working on the local stations, working as shepherds and stockman. In this way they were still able to keep their very strong bonds with the tribal lands from which they had otherwise been displaced.

After the Ghan had arrived in Arabana country in 1884, Baldwin Spencer and Francis Gillen's later writings from 1912 indicate a further reduction in numbers of Arabana. They say "the remnants of the Urabunna [sic] are gathered together at the few outlying cattle stations...they help in the work of the station". In fact the station would have been impossible to run without cheap Aboriginal labour, as Gillen noted as far back as 1875 (as quoted above). "They have long since, except in a very small way, given up the performance of their old ceremonies – even the ordinary corroborees have dwindled down to a mere nothing – and only the older men know anything about, or indeed take any interest in, matters of tribal lore" (Spencer and Gillen 1912). Even if true, the reasons for this are not given. Whether it was just a matter of concealment from the inquisitive outsider, or whether Spencer's statement is true we have no way of knowing. If true, then not bullets, but bacteria may be a likely explanation. Arabana whom I talked to, by way of contrast, say that the last full initiations of Arabana men took place in the 1950s at Curdimurka.

The worldwide pandemic of influenza in 1918-19 had killed a lot of Aboriginal Australians in this region, an all too common aspect of globalisation. The death rate was much higher for Aboriginal Australians than white people in Australia. Other diseases were rife such as the somewhat earlier smallpox, tuberculosis, measles, venereal disease and so on. Children and elders were especially vulnerable. It is possible that body lice and typhus carried by the workers and passengers on the Ghan also impacted upon Arabana numbers, although direct evidence is lacking. Diphtheria and whooping cough (pertussis) need to be added as likely high killers of children.

Child Removals

Then there was an active policy of child removal particularly of "half-caste" children starting in the twentieth century under new legislation after World War 1. Even earlier, John Warren (the second), in his role as a Member of the Legislative Council, had asked questions (South Australian Parliamentary Papers 1911) about removal of children. The fathers, you may be sure, were not necessarily Aboriginal Australians. Moreover, at this time in history, no Arabana person was likely to have English writing skills. It was not long after this that more draconian provisions were passed by the Parliament to control the movements and associations of Aboriginal people throughout South Australia. Instead of dying out, the Aboriginal and particularly "half-caste" population was increasing! Arabana still moved around their own country.

Still later, the UAM established a Mission at Oodnadatta on Arabana territory in 1926. This moved some children away from their parents who were frequently not returned. They also established in 1929 another new mission at Nepabunna, east of Copley, which was a special place of the local Andyamathanha. Later, Arabana children, such as subsequent Korean War veteran Steve Dodd, were sent to Colebrook in Quorn, out of country. When that last alleged "full blood" died in 1973, so it is said that ended the handing down of special dreaming stories that could only be handed down to fully initiated members of the tribe. Eileen Wingfield, however, told me that she is teaching one of her daughters some stories associated with the Seven Sisters Dreaming.

Basedow's Third Medical Relief Expedition 1920 examined 850 Aborigines from Marree to Hermannsburg and found very poor health among the living, and greatly excessive mortality. Basedow, with his team and equipment, arrived by special train in Marree – one of the many uses of the Ghan. Some 65 Arabana were examined and their personal details recorded. The train line is not mentioned with regard to Arabana people themselves – all are examined on pastoral stations. The Arabana and other Aboriginal Australians were supposed to be kept away from the railway by then, so it was perhaps just politeness or tact by Basedow that he did not mention the Aboriginal Australians proximate to the line, as many informants have told me they were.

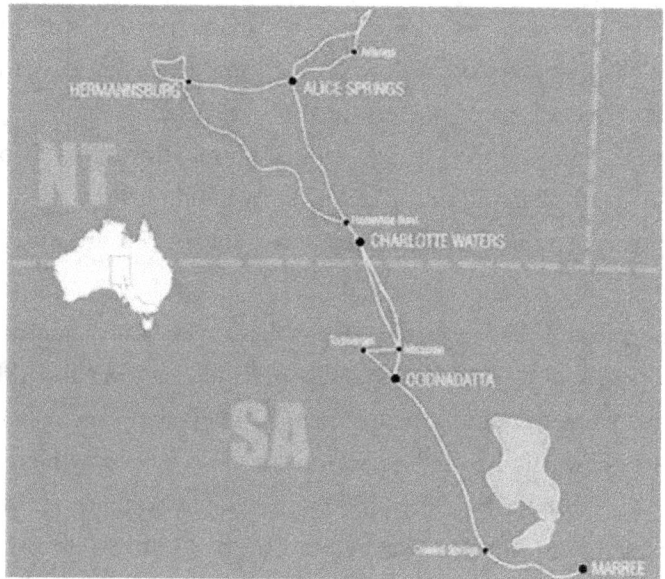

Route of Dr Herbert Basedow's Third Medical Relief Expedition: May 1920

The Highly Regarded Francis Dunbar Warren

Francis Dunbar Warren (who only died in 1958), seventh and youngest son of John Warren (3/9/1830 to 13/9/1914) of Strangways, the son of John Warren of Springfield, Mount Crawford (established in the 1840s), moved to re-establish Finniss Springs Station, moving from Anna Creek in the post-World War I period and to "New Well" in 1922. He was the landholder together with William Wood. With F. D. Warren were his partner, an Arabana woman named Laura Beralda (sometimes spelt Paralta), and later their children. Under the *1911 Aborigines Act* such relations between and a white and an Aboriginal Australian were illegal but as with many matters, the law and people's behaviour do not necessarily coincide.

Other Aboriginal Australians joined the Arabana later. For instance, when Killalpannina Mission in Dieri country closed in 1915 (partly due to anti-German sentiment in the First World War), some came to Finniss Springs Station. Similarly, when the Oodnadatta Mission closed in the 1940s, some Arrernte moved to Finniss Springs too. When severe droughts occurred, other Aborigines moved in from even more desert regions.

Francis Dunbar Warren employed mostly Aboriginal people and encouraged them to live in family units at the homestead. At a time when Aboriginal Australian and especially part-Aboriginal children were routinely removed from their families to receive a European education, Warren refused to allow the Finniss Springs children to be taken away. Initially he had no way of providing them an education, as he was reluctant to allow churches to become involved in Finniss Springs, fearing they would want too much control.

Buzzacott, Wood and Dodd Families

Warren's Aboriginal wife, Bralda (as noted, also known as Laura, or Baralda and as Nora Beralda or Paralta) bore thirteen children. His eldest daughter was called Merna, also known as Mona or Lena. Some of the others, as recalled by Reg Dodd, were his mother Amy, Flora and two sons, Arthur and Angus.

Amy married an Arrente man Alan Buzzacott (the surname is spelt "Bossicott" by the linguist Luise Hercus), and later bore Reg Dodd and other children. Amy had been married before to Thomas Dodd. She also had children to Bill Wood, the co-owner with Francis Dunbar Warren. As the Arabana have been matrilineal from pre-colonial times so the mother was the clear descent line as recognised by the Arabana themselves.

By the 1930s there was a large Aboriginal community living at the Finniss Springs station homestead, possibly 400 people. Initial contact with F. D. Warren for a Mission was rejected, as noted, but he subsequently consented and gave much practical help. He contracted with Andrew Pearce of the United Aborigines Mission to open a school at Finniss Springs in 1939. At first an all-purpose brush shed was built and school began in March 1939 with sixteen children.

The Mission school at Finniss Springs Station. Dated unknown.

Then wood and iron were ordered for a missionaries room and school was transferred to their tent, which had to be lowered in storms in case it was torn apart. Soon concrete blocks were moulded on the site by the Arabana themselves and a combined school and church was built by 1940. F.D. Warren gave permission for this to occur because it meant that the people could remain together in one place.

There was some fear among these "station blacks" of Kokatha parties coming down the Deep Creek which runs through the Station especially at night to seek revenge for perceived slights or magical deaths, to steal women or the like.

The Second World War did not take Arabana away to fight as soldiers for the Allies. There was one man, Frank Churches, who was seen in a military uniform by the Hodgson family, but his history is unknown. Some continued either as pastoral employees albeit usually with trivial wages, or backfilled other roles. Attitudes had not necessarily improved towards Aboriginal Australians. Constable Collins of the Marree Police Station wrote to Inspector Parsonage, the "Protector of Aboriginals", on 15th July 1942: "...I have had several enquiries from drovers and Stations regarding working aboriginals [sic], these as you are already aware receive wages, and it is generally recognised that whilst they are employed it is the duty of their respective owners to provide adequate clothing and food...". "Owners": slavery had been abolished in the British Empire a century before, in theory. They were at best akin to indentured labourers, there to serve the needs of their pastoral overlords.

In the Second World War, a number of Arabana were riding flat-top rail cars which were sandbagged at each end and fitted with guns to defend trains from possible Japanese attack. It is a far cry from the earlier possible threat to use police or troops brought up by train against Arabana or other Aboriginal Australians.

Control of Arabana by police representing the Aborigines Protection Board continued to be draconian and micromanaging. The same letter from Constable Collins cited above has the heartless refusal to allow a nearly blind Aboriginal lady, Ruby Murray (the wife of Arabana man Arthur Warren), to have Arabana Ida Stewart as an accompanying person take her to the hospital in Port Augusta from Marree on the Ghan. This was despite a supportive letter from Mrs Pearce, wife of the Missionary Alexander Pearce at Finniss Springs. The UAM now clearly supported the ideas of F. D. Warren about more egalitarian human-human relationships. Clearly some tension between Mission and the local authorities existed. The same Constable Collins did give Finniss Springs people Bertha and George Murray single (not return) tickets to get to Port Augusta Hospital from Alberrie Creek when Mrs Murray was clearly very pregnant and quite ill.

Rations of tobacco, flour, rice, sugar and tea were being approved by the Aborigines' Protection Board, but in small amounts, as all able-bodied Aboriginal Australians were expected to be working and were said to be "well paid" (GRG52/1, 1924 report). Golden Syrup and Baking Powder were also supplied in small amounts. The situation was the same in the 1940s (GRG52/1, 1943 report). There was, however, "no need for clothing" to be supplied (GRG52/1, 1st August 1944 letter), suggesting either that the Aboriginal Australians were supposed to remain naked or that employers were supposed to supply workers and their families with clothes. Or that they bought clothing from those "good wages". On the railways, clothes and other supplies came on order from the store at Port Augusta. On 9th May 1946, however, second hand clothing was to be sent to the Police at Marree for distribution.

Moreover, Aboriginal Australians working on sheep or cattle

stations also had no mechanism of getting clothing, tobacco etc except by the station holder appealing to the Aborigines' Protection Board, quite different from the railway workers at the same time. So in reality, the Arabana at Anna Creek and Finniss Springs were at the mercy of the Board and the Warrens who controlled all aspects of their lives. Fortunately, in the case of the latter, however, it was a benign dictatorship, paternalistic but fondly regarded by all his current descendants.

By 1948, the local landholders were prepared to "dob" in others who were mistreating their Arabana employees. In an expurgated letter of 17th September, Ernest Murray of Murnpeowie Station states that Henry Rowlands has been flogged and imprisoned without food or water on Clifton Hills Station by Mr and Mrs Rowlands, land-holders.

By 1950 the Flying Doctor Service was visiting Marree directly and would recommend, for instance, rail transfers on the Ghan to Hospital at Hawker or Port Augusta. The Police still had to approve such travel and seek confirmation from the Aborigines' Protection Board. The Mission and school continued until the late 1950s then were replaced by a UAM School in Marree in 1965. Finniss Springs had struggled due to the lack of water and eventually people could not continue just carting water for their needs (Aborigines Protection Board Report 1960).

When F. D. Warren died in 1958 he was not allowed to bequeath the Station to his Aboriginal children. Nonetheless, the property passed to his Arabana son, Arthur Warren. Like his father, Arthur had married an Indigenous women, Rosa Murray, who was a Dieri woman, in September 1941 at the Finniss Springs Mission school. Arthur faced insurmountable odds in managing the station. Arthur ended his working life as manager of Maree's Railway Rest House. When he died in 1989, he was survived by four daughters and three sons. Stan Warren, youngest son of Francis Dunbar Warren with Laura, however, states that he ran the station for a number of years after F. D. Warren's death.

When a TB survey was done at the end of 1959, there were 292 Aboriginal Australians living up and down the Ghan line. Initiations were still occurring: Gale (1964) writes "a young half-caste from Marree was encouraged by older men to go north to Anna Creek, to be made into a 'young fella'".

Micromanagement did continue. For instance on 12th May 1960, Constable Neale at Marree requested and was given permission by the Aborigines' Protection Board to buy a load of firewood, cost not to exceed 5 pounds. Rail passes continued to be required for any Aboriginal Australian travelling by the train.

The dispossessing pastoral prequel to the establishment of the railway had already allowed Arabana people to interact with, adapt to and cause adaptations from the white people. It would appear that Finniss Springs and the earlier Strangways had been paternalistic but relatively benign in intent and deed by the standards of the time. Against the backdrop of global changes including Federation, the formation of Commonwealth Railways, World War II and decolonisation movements worldwide, nonetheless Arabana had gross limits until they engaged in employment with the Railways. As for many Aboriginal Australians, employment on the railways offered social mobility, and the opportunities to travel and trade with the broader settler society.

Section of abandoned track cutting through Finniss.
(Photograph courtesy of Susan SP Dodd)

3

FROM SONGLINES TO TRAINLINES

"Architecture ... power made visible"
(Hitchens, 2010, p 39)

Early Railways In SA

The Colony of South Australia was just 11 years old when railways became a political issue. The success of the English in setting up commercial railways powered by steam locomotives from 1826 had excited interest in Europe and people all around the world interested in "progress". The first ordinance or Act of Parliament regulating the construction of railways in South Australia was passed in March 1847. The Railways Clauses Consolidation Act (No 7 of 1847) did not authorise the construction of any specific railway but outlined the conditions under which any companies seeking such a right could undertake the tasks. The actual construction of any specific railway required further Acts for each separate length of railway.

The financiers and engineers responsible for these constructions were no respecter of persons. As the building of landmark London railway stations and their rail lines occurred, 120,000 people were displaced from their houses between 1840 and 1900 without recompense. These were white people at the Empire's core, displaced for "progress". This did not augur well for those Aboriginal populations of South Australia whose traditional lands were seen as being required for the construction of railway lines.

Aboriginal Australians Off The Train Of Progress

This ruthlessness was seen in the State of Victoria where railways started to be built in 1854. By that time, Victoria had become a separate colony, gold had been discovered and pastoral enterprises were widespread. Travel by foot and horse drawn coach was manifestly inadequate. Nonetheless, the Argus (12th September 1854), usually thought of as a conservative newspaper, suggests that not all of the inhabitants of that State would welcome the railway innovation.

Torrens Bridge, Adelaide. Henry Glover 1856

The train, according to the paper, would "flash past the gunya of the native black" filling him or her with "wonder" or "vague terror". The train symbolised "*Christian* England, the great, the powerful, the intelligent, the good!". The newspaper spoke of the other side of white progress - the stealing of Aboriginal lands, "destroy(*ing*) your game", it will "inoculate you with her vices". "*Christian* England" will shew her Christian spirit by dooming you to 'extirpation'". Ironically *The Argus* concludes "Rejoice, you dark-skinned savage, at the advent of your kind, magnanimous, and *most Christian brother*".

Early horse-drawn railways were opened at the same time in South Australia to the south of Adelaide, the land of the Kaurna people, the Peramangk and the Ngarrindjeri without recompense. Indicative of the exclusion of Aboriginal people from their own lands is a poignant reminder in *A History of the South Australian Railways* written by Stewien and Thompson in 2007. On the cover is a picture by Henry Glover showing Torrens Bridge in 1856. A group of Aborigines is depicted in the foreground, looking up at the train and the white settlement on the hill. The area north of the river was known from 1837 to 1845 as the Native Location. In the centre of the painting is the Iron Store, one of the few Native Location buildings still standing in 1856. A few Aboriginal people continued to live in the area after 1845 but the majority had left or died by the time of Glover's painting. It had become a painterly tradition to have Aborigines, like decorative fauna, in pictures of the Australian landscape, and Glover is no exception, painting the natives as marginal figures, and off the train of "progress".

First Train in South Australia

Building Railways To The North Of South Australia: Beginnings Of The Ghan

Part of the pastoral expansion into the north of South Australia involved the dream of construction of a railway. This would enable stock to be rapidly and safely transported to markets, goods such as coal and wheat to be moved to ports, and labour to be quickly available from the metropole to mining and agricultural regions. In case of a threat from any quarter, the railway would also be able to transport troops or police rapidly to the trouble spot. Moreover the idea of linking southern and northern parts of the continent gained "steam" when the fears of invasion from "Asian hordes" as well as other European powers escalated. Joining Adelaide and Palmerston, later called Darwin, was the original aim, not achieved for 120 years after the Central Australian Railway was started. Prior to that, the line, even under Australian Commonwealth control, had terminated at Alice Springs with nearly a 1,000 Km gap to Birdum in the Northern Territory.

PORT AUGUSTA TO ALICE SPRINGS

ALICE SPRINGS

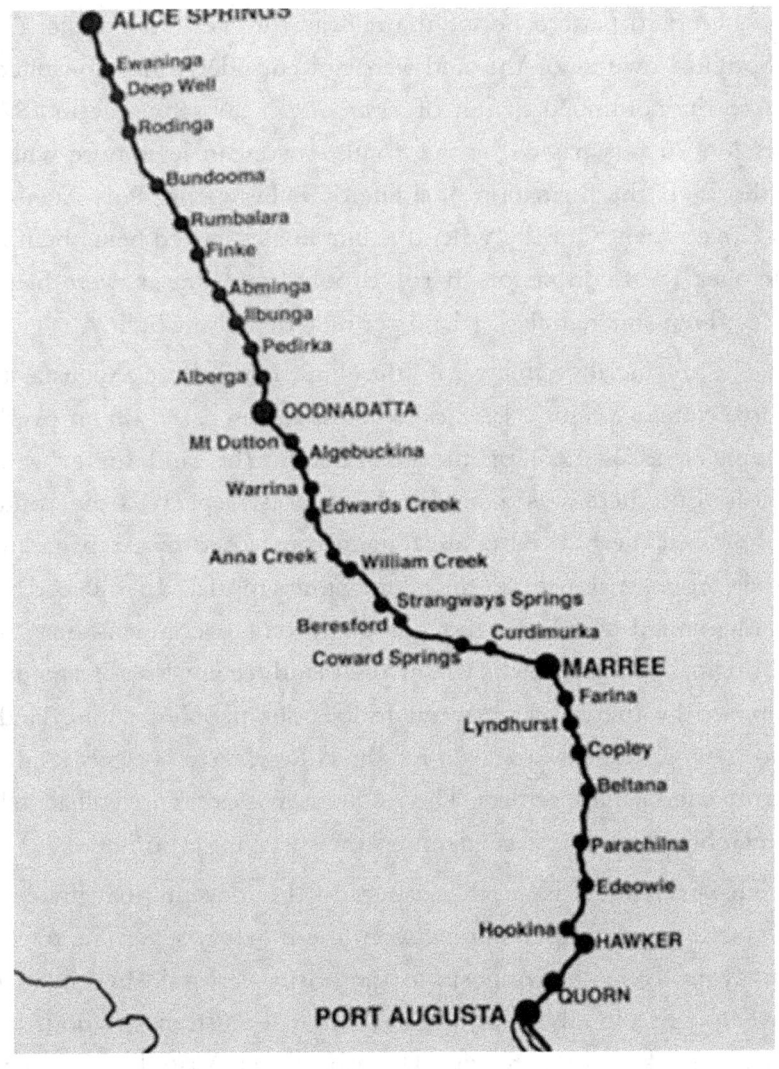

The Old Ghan Route

The Old Ghan Route

In 1862 the Port Augusta and Overland Railways Act was passed by the South Australian Parliament. Railway building contractors were offered two square miles then four square miles of land in a chequerboard pattern beside the railway for every mile built. The Aboriginal owners of the land were not considered nor consulted, under the continued fiction of *terra nullius*. Subsequently in 1876 Act No 26 was passed by the South Australian legislature which authorised "the formation of a line of railway from Port Augusta to Government Gums". When the line finally started being built in October 1878 contractors Barry, Brookes and Fraser, were being offered ten square miles of land per mile of railway built.

The financial viability of the line from Port Augusta to "Government Gums", later called Farina, was based on an overly optimistic assessment of the potential of the land for growing wheat. But there was a hidden Indigenous aspect to the route. It followed the old red ochre trading route used by Arabana and other Aboriginal people since time immemorial. In those days, as mentioned above, no thought was given to compensating the Aboriginal peoples for the use of their land for any loss of amenity imposed by the railway. Several Indigenous peoples, whose lands and trading routes were taken for the railway, were savagely treated by the encroaching settlers. The resultant massacres are still acutely remembered by the descendants of the surviving Aborigines.

However, there is another aspect to these events that involves interaction and cooperation between these two groups. The track's surveyors from Port Augusta to the north were said by Fuller to have sought the advice of local Aboriginal Australians about the ancient tracks of the region. The Aboriginal Australians' trading and ceremonial routes were known by white pioneers to skirt areas prone to flooding, and this was imparted to the surveyors. So, in considerable part, the railway survey was shaped by the paths once taken by the red-ochre traders and pilgrims.

Aboriginal trading camps were spaced at intervals of about 100 miles. One of these camps was on the site of the present-day Marree. Here the coloured clays were exchanged for shields, spear shafts and other material unobtainable in the Flinders Ranges and southern regions. The red-ochre track continued northwards following the future route of the railway through Parachilna and the Hergott Springs (later called Marree) district. Afterwards it struck north-eastwards to Boulia, with a branch snaking through Kopperamanna to Charleville. When barter was completed visiting parties of never more than three strong left at once, with each man carrying on his head a block of ochre weighing up to fifty pounds (about 25Kg). Work on this section of the complex narrow-gauge rail route from Port Augusta to Farina took a remarkably short span of three years. Aboriginal Australians are not recorded as members of the construction gangs. It seems likely that the settlers treated them as obstructions. As Deborah Rose Bird, in paraphrase, has said, all Indigenous people had to do to be in the way was stay at home. Nor would the Aboriginal Australians have necessarily welcomed further incursions onto their traditional lands.

Once the line from Port Augusta to Farina had been completed with the official opening on 17th May 1882, the next phase from Farina to Hergott Springs, the later named Marree, was immediately put out to tender. It had been authorised by a new Act, No 226 on 18th November 1881, similar to that of 1876. Again the contractors were to be awarded ten square miles of land adjacent to the railway line for each mile of track built. New contractors, Moorhouse, Robinson and Jesser won the contract and work started on 10th

November 1882 in Farina. On 6th January 1884 the railway reached Hergott Springs, a town proclaimed just two months before, and in October 1884 the railway station was finished. It included a running shed large enough for an engine and tender and two carriages; a goods shed, sixty feet by forty-five feet; staff offices; and a large water-tank for the supply of locomotives. Until this time, locomotive water had been obtained from a pipe leading across country from the Hergott Springs. An artesian bore, 140 feet deep and five and a half inches in diameter, was sunk for railway use. This bore was situated within the railway enclosure and, since, under its own pressure, water rose from the piping to a height of sixty-four feet, the tank, some 200 yards distant, could be supplied without the use of a pump. So the spring itself, which was known to Arabana as "the snake's earhole", was only used for 10 months before the bore was sunk. A great irony, as had the bore been sunk earlier, the spring area could have been left alone. A rail route directly across country from Farina to Callana would have left the Marree trading hub alone. As it was, the Aboriginal people's traditional watering place was encroached upon and then white settlement stayed. Though the railway was an initial source of exclusion, it did become a further means by which the Arabana, in particular, began to interact with the dominant settler economy and in particular beyond pastoral servitude.

Aboriginal Australians Working On The Railway

Almost immediately at Hergott Springs, Marree, the local Aboriginal people were employed by the railway. After the bore had been sunk, a coaling stage was built close to the water-tank. The practice was to carry coal in large baskets from a bulk store in the yard. When full, a basket weighed eighty-four pounds (about 38Kg). Raised to the platform by means of a hand-operated hoist, it was emptied by hand into the waiting tender. One hundred and thirty baskets were needed to fill a small tender. To manhandle this quantity of coal required two hours of hard, sweating toil.

Along the length of the line it became the custom for train crews to pay Aboriginal Australians to do this heavy manual work. The practice was popular with station staffs who were supposed to assist in coaling. Apparently it was popular with the Aboriginal Australians too, for they are said to have delighted in working the hoist. Mainly Arabana and Kuyani in that area, they would have been employed on a walk-up basis. They were paid usually in food and tobacco. It seems logical that they had known the railway was coming for several years from their neighbours and their own observations as they made pilgrimages south for the ochre. The records of the employment of staff for the railway from 1858 to 1913 do not have any names of such early-employed Aborigines. Such employment was invisible to the official records. And the paid staff would discount these efforts. Moreover, the history of this work did not even pass down to subsequent generations of Arabana.

Marree To Oodnadatta

Urged on by pastoralists, and funded by land sales, the next stage of building of the railway was directly on Arabana country from Marree to Oodnadatta. The rail route between Marree and Oodnadatta is far from direct. Why did the train line take that course? As steam trains need water, and lots of it the question arose of where could water be found in that seemingly bleak landscape? The Arabana people knew. Arabana had guided the German-born artist and surveyor Herrgott and his colleagues and "explorers" such as Stuart to the mound springs where copious amounts of water could be found. Some of these, it is admitted, stand out as green beacons in a desolate landscape, but some are much more subtle. John McDouall Stuart's diaries, for example, record many Aboriginal tracks and trails leading him and his party to water, springs, waterholes and so on. These were not animal pads, but Arabana tracks. Any Aborigine living a traditional lifestyle could disguise or obliterate tracks, so this was deliberate.

Coaling before 1922
(Jennings, 1973, with permission)

The educationalist and geographer Charles Fenner himself also stated that the decision to take the railway to Oodnadatta was greatly influenced by the "discovery" of the presence of mound springs along the south-western border of the Great Artesian Basin. As Fenner pointed out the distribution of pastoral population and the location of stock routes was related to the artesian basin springs, which rise from great depth through fissures in a fault that occurs where the floor of Lake Eyre basin meets ancient rock to the west. Thus springs such as Blanche Cup (*'Dirga', the oven*), the Bubbler (*'Bidilina', snake's writhing*) and other free-flowing springs providing completely reliable supplies influenced the advice that the railway surveyors, guided by Arabana, gave the Government in the matter of the route to be followed by the railway.

On 26th September 1883, the South Australian legislature passed Act No 281 authorising the building of the line of railway from Hergott Springs to Primrose Springs (east of the present Algebuckina, see endpaper map). This latter, Primrose Springs, has the Arabana name *Papu-ngaljuru* (Blue Egg); it was a large mound spring set amid sandhills north of the Neales River. It was well known and used by Arabana in pre-colonial times. Because of a local economic downturn, so it was said, the Government itself decided to run the building project rather than contract it out to external contractors. Building the rail line north of Marree from 1884 to 1891 was undertaken mainly by formerly unemployed white men, partly because of a recession in white South Australian society at the time. It was not without risk. I came across in the Marree cemetery a memorial to five workers killed at the Finniss on 21st April 1886, during construction of the next section of the line to William Creek.

Not having external contractors also meant that there was no necessary hand-out of land to anybody during the section from Hergott Springs to Oodnadatta. How extraordinary: the only part of the old Ghan line where land was not handed out *gratis* to white contractors was Arabana country! Construction started on 16th July 1884. Use of unskilled labour rather than regular navvies, however, meant that the building of the line went much more slowly than the previous two phases. The Government use of its own labour force saved the Strangways and other pastoral properties from being resumed for the railway contractors.

Tribute in Marree Cemetery erected to the memory of five men killed building the Marree to Oodnadatta section of the railway. This was an industrial accident not Aboriginal violence

Shaw notes families of Ah Kits and Ah Chees at Oodnadatta from early times so some Chinese/Arabana people did work upon this construction. Labourers were paid on a daily basis; it was only station masters and the like who had annual salaries.

The various Arabana families through whose land the new railway line passed were, of course, not compensated, nor even considered. I could not find records of any Arabana people employed on the train line during the Marree to Oodnadatta construction years, 1884-1891. Professor Veronica Arbon, Arabana elder and academic, told me, however, that Arabana, working as stockmen on Strangways Springs Station, supplied meat to the railway construction teams. By that time, as noted in the previous chapter, many Arabana were living on pastoral stations or "runs" which had been taken up, expropriated, by the white settlers since 1862. The semi-feudal life of working on pastoral properties, recorded in histories by Frank Stevens in 1974 and Dawn May in 1994 and others, was being lived by most Arabana. Nonetheless, the Arabana had realized that there were benefits to be gained from these infra structure projects. For instance, the Overland Telegraph Line, which had been put through between 1870 and 1872, had introduced Arabana living more traditional lives and using stone tools to the joys of ceramics and glass for sharp implements. Even here, compromise and recognition of differing needs seems to have prevailed.

Marree had police from 1882, two years before the arrival of the railway, but ten years after the Overland Telegraph. The construction workers on the railway further north, however, were thought to require the presence of another police station, which was established on Strangways Station in 1886 through to 1888. It would seem that these railway construction workers were suspected to become disruptive so necessitating a police station in the middle of the railway construction between Marree and Oodnadatta. Evidence of actual disruptiveness, however, does not appear in the available police records. Five to six hundred men lived in tents about 2 Km north of the Strangways repeater station. Temporary structures such as Bennett's Eating House and Store were established. There were sheds for clerks and tents for a butcher and saddler. Even a hotel was built in 1886 and sly grog sales were part of the police role to deter. Race meetings and the inevitable gambling kept the men entertained. The nearby Arabana pastoral workers kept a close eye on these novelties. The police were there to control the construction crews, not the Arabana. There was a further police station built at Peake Station, further north on Arabana land. Both these police stations were abandoned when Oodnadatta became the new railhead in 1891 and the rail construction teams were no longer present.

Aboriginal Australians' marginal status is poignantly emphasised in Professor John Gregory's account of his expedition. Appointed Professor of Geology at the University of Melbourne in 1899, he led an expedition to central Australia in the summer of 1901-2 and has left a lively account in his 1906 book *The Dead Heart of Australia*. He travelled by train to Marree, then still called Hergott Springs, and gives a description of the town at that time just after the turn of the century. He emphasises the camelmen who were ubiquitous, as Hergott was the terminus for the stock and trade route to southwest Queensland, where no railway ran. He adds "Until recently all communications to the back blocks of Queensland, even the customs' books and police officers, were sent from Brisbane via Melbourne and Hergott, a journey of 2,553 miles, including 330 miles by cart, to reach a place only 530 miles from a station on the Queensland railways". Although he describes the place as dreary, he does admit it has a beauty of its own. "The pure colours at dawn and sunset, ... the thatched, mud-walled huts of the Afghan camp and its turbaned inhabitants, all give the country an Oriental aspect".

Gregory hired Aboriginal guides "from time to time" but no names, let alone tribal names, are given. He does not mention the Arabana inhabitants of Marree itself. Later in the book, however, he gives a detailed description of his views of the "Lake Eyre Aborigines" (p166235). To his credit he disdainfully dismisses and refutes the racist speculations of various writers who had described the Aboriginal Australians as "the zero ... of all anthropological analysis". He writes "Instead of finding them degraded, lazy, selfish, savage, they were courteous and intelligent, generous even to the point of imprudence, and phenomenally honest; while in the field, they proved to be born naturalists and superb bushmen". Gregory also managed to observe a corroboree at the Peake Station near the Neales River which must have had Arabana participants (1906, p210-221), as this is part of their traditional lands. Gregory either does not see or does not record involvement with the railway of Aboriginal Australians he meets.

Terminus of the Great Northern Railway, Oodnadatta. 1905
(Photograph Courtesy of the State Library of South Australia [B 11733])

He does not mention the Aboriginal Australians who had gravitated to Marree or the railway sidings, or those who had established relationships with white men, although this could be because he supported the idea of segregation.

Charles Kunoth, writing in 1988, grew up on Muloorina Station at the south end of Lake Eyre on Frome Creek from 1908 to 1920 then was in Marree for the ensuing ten years. He says that even in the 1920s "Aboriginals in those days preferred to live their own lifestyle" (p23).

This, as we have seen, was grossly untrue given the appropriation, subjugation of sovereignty and introduction of alien animals which they were not allowed to hunt; travel was constrained and pastoral life the norm for many. He also has a vivid description of a train trip undertaken on the Old Ghan from Oodnadatta to Marree in the early twentieth century (p43-44): "There was a timetable but no one knew where it was or cared. Only the day was known. When it (the train) left Oodnadatta an engine would be fired up at William Creek in case of a breakdown. It took about four hours for a steam engine to get up enough steam to work it. On arriving at William Creek lunch would be served in the dining room of what was then the wine saloon for anyone wanting a meal. On the side of the carriages written in chalk would be 'ladies and children's carriage, 'drunks's carriage', 'smoking carriage' etc. From the tanks on top of the passengers' carriages there was water for toilets and hand basins."

Cattle train of 22 vans about to leave Oodnadatta with 250 head for the Adelaide Market in 1927
(Photograph Courtesy of the State Library of South Australia [B 53587])

Professor Alistair Paterson, who worked on archaeological digs at Strangways Station in the late 1990s as written about above, mentions the railway on several occasions in his 2008 book, *The Lost Legions*. For pastoralists, he says on page 167, the railway was a great boon. It enabled stock to be transported faster and more safely to markets.

Instead of six to eight miles a day with cattle, they could be moved at thirty miles an hour! This shrinks the distance, in terms of time, thirtyfold. It also meant that drovers' time could be minimised, which meant lower labour costs, a critical consideration for those marginal farms. Cattle or sheep also arrived in better condition at the sale yards in Adelaide.

The further interactions between the railway construction teams and the Arabana are not recorded, but it is indisputable that Aboriginal people congregated around railway sidings once they were built, until regulation was passed to try and preclude this in 1927 during the time when the line was being extended further north. The line had been laid as far as Oodnadatta by 7th January 1891 but took another thirty-eight years to reach Alice Springs on 2nd August 1929, the hiatus being mainly for financial reasons - the South Australian Government nearly beggared itself with large-scale public works such as the Overland Telegraph Line and the Great Northern Railway/Central Australian Railway. During this long interval Oodnadatta was the depot and terminus. Over that long time Arabana people came and settled in the town or around it. As noted above there was no enforced prohibitive legislation, as there was in other States, until the 1920s.

There is a relative dearth of written sources about the ensuing years from 1891 until the 1950s. *"Beltana - Six Miles"* from Payne in 1974 is a perhaps unreliable exception. "Beltana" means "running water" in the local language. In this account, written by the daughter of a white fettler about the years between 1899 and the First World War, Aboriginal Australians are peripheral. They are seen laughing outside a dance hall where Europeans are celebrating. One is visited as he is "boned" and his transfer to a hospital is arranged. Nothing else. The Aboriginal people were essential workers but lived lives in different accommodation with ongoing traditional beliefs and behaviours.

South Australian MP Simpson Mara Newland, in a book published in 1926, went to England in 1906 to raise money to further extend the railway. He, incidentally, wrote a sympathetic account of Aboriginal people being mistreated and massacred as white people defended the Overland Telegraph Line, in *Blood Tracks in the Bush* (1900). Disconcertingly, the South Australian Government rejected Newland's international fund-raising efforts and the subsequent World War I between 1914 and 1918 increased the State's debt so nothing came of his ideas. Arabana in their own expropriated lands were not involved in any of this and there is no record of their serving in the military in World War 1. Despite his sympathies and personal involvement with both Ngarrindjeri and Barkindji peoples, Newland, a one-time treasurer in the Downer Ministry of the 1880s, did not consult the Arabana.

Even after World War I, the influenza pandemic and with high interest rates, the South Australian Parliament believed "no railways, no progress". But only uneconomic lines were built until the late 1920s by the State, a subject scathingly written about by former rail worker Dr Reece Jennings.

Given the loss of their land, the railways provided sources of food for the Arabana and other Indigenous peoples, and the Arabana settled in and around the towns. New types of relationships were formed between the Arabana and white settlers and workers. The Arabana were offered work, performing menial tasks on a sporadic basis, and intermarriage occurred. Many non-Aboriginal workers on the railways and telegraph line, or connected to the pastoral and cameleer industries, married Arabana women. Before the introduction of legislation restricting Aboriginal Australians' movements in the 1920s, there were no prohibitions on their movements or behaviour, as there were in other states. But there were concerns for the welfare of the "race". With numbers estimated to have reduced nationally to 60,000 in 1920, Aboriginal Australians were considered by most white Australians as 'a dying race' One egregious example of this false idea was expressed by the respondents to an endowment by Lady Henrietta Smith of Dunesk in Scotland. She laid aside money to buy land in the South Australian colony to help the Aboriginal Australians. The Colonial Committee of the Free Church of Scotland in 1853 specifically advised her that this would be useless as the Aboriginal Australians were a dying race. As we know this false idea was ascarcely disguised wish that this was true, or would become so with "the logic of elimination".

Bruce Plowman, a missionary from 1914 to 1917 Oodnadatta circa 1914. (Photograph Courtesy of the State Library of South Australia [B 61841])

In reality the churches were involved throughout the colonial period. Robert Bruce Plowman was the padre for a huge area in Central Australia but based at Oodnadatta for many years. He has written two books of his experiences, *The Man from Oodnadatta* (1933) and *Camel Pads* (1935). The former describes a trip to the Northern Territory out of Arabana land but the latter has quite a lot of information about Oodnadatta itself and the train line. For instance he describes the arrival of the fortnightly train in an un-named year before the extension to Alice Springs, so before 1926, in vivid and amusing terms. Everybody in town made some excuse to come and visit the station to enquire when the train may arrive. Replies grew more and more terse as the day wore on and no arrival had occurred. Plowman also notes the Camelmen: as this was the end of the railway line for those thirty-eight years from 1891 to 1929, all supplies henceforward went by camel train. He concludes this section with the excitement of the train coming in.

"By seven o'clock odd groups of bushmen and children began to form near the station-building. By seven-thirty half Oodnadatta was there. At eight o'clock the only residents missing were the hotel and boarding-house staffs – prevented from being present by the necessity of having meals ready for the train's passengers – and old Dicky. The very young children were there in their mothers' arms or hanging on to their skirts. Older children raced around, filling in time until the moment of major excitement arrived. The eyes of the adults kept turning towards a rise some miles down the track where they could catch the first sight of smoke in summer, or of the engine's lamps in winter. "Here she comes!" someone would call; and all Oodnadatta – the padre and the Sister included – congregated on the space between the buildings and the rails which was dignified by the name of platform to greet the train, its crew, and especially its passengers."

So the Christian padre was very much part of the white establishment in Oodnadatta, and seems to have felt the "Afghans" and Aboriginal Australians were relatively apart from his parish. He had a "black boy" of his own called Dick Gillen and another reluctant and truculent one called George. In *The Man From Oodnadatta* Dick Gillen is very much part of the padre's camel expedition around his 160,000 square miles parish north of the train line, but the only Aboriginal Australians we meet on the circuit are a "quadroon" ("quarter-caste") who is marrying a bashful Aboriginal bride. In *Camel Pads* he meets many others but generally describes the Aboriginal Australians to the west of Oodnadatta as "wholly uncivilised and treacherous" (for objecting to white occupation of their land).

Nonetheless, there they were, the Aboriginal Australians, in the township, and getting rations. Employment of this group in the town itself just after the First World War seems not to be prevalent, except as helpers to the "Afghans". Plowman describes a lady from this area as a "camp lubra". Elsewhere in the book Plowman writes of Harry Gepp, the storekeeper, who is said to have been a camel driver of the Inland in the past. Gepp describes to Plowman that "the blacks" as "very bad in those days as there weren't many whites about" and also says "Sometimes even when we go to water we couldn't camp on account of the blacks". Whether this was in Arabana country or elsewhere is not made clear. And wishing he'd had a partner, Harry says, "Of course, I had a team of black boys, but you know a man can't talk to them". Now Gepp is a very common Arabana surname, so Mr Harry Gepp almost certainly did have at least one "mate" and either the Aboriginal people called Gepp are descendants or just named themselves after the white man, as did the Strangways family. Once a storeman, however, Gepp acquired a white wife from town and a "black boy" called "Gepp's Charlie".

Plowman also writes of several train journeys including one by a nursing sister on a railway tricycle travelling 127 miles to William Creek to nurse a very sick boy through the night. His own excursions included taking a sick man to the Port Augusta Hospital (three days with overnight stops in Marree and Quorn) and a memorable trip with increasingly drunken navvies who had acquired their alcohol at Coward Springs. More grimly he also writes of "black prisoners": "Slowly advancing towards the township from the west was a remarkable procession. At its head were six naked blackfellows, four of them fastened together by chains attached to a central plate of iron, two in front and two behind. Beside them were two more, one in front and one in the rear. The outside two were chained neck to neck and each was handcuffed to the blackfellow on his left. Behind the six walked a blacktracker with a rifle over his shoulder. There followed about a dozen naked and unchained blacks, a police trooper and another white man riding side by side on camels, several pack- camels led by a black boy, and, tailing in the rear, a mixed mob of lubras, piccaninnies friends and relations of the two groups of blackfellows up in front."

Prisoners were transported to Port Augusta on the Ghan line and often housed overnight in the Marree Police Station on the way, with all meals and lodging paid for by the Aborigines' Protection Board (one pound for four men on 23rd May 1934 for two days and nights, for instance, not a large amount.

Plowman gives no more details and just relates his own apprehension about visiting that area. In the same book, Plowman has other references to the critically important train line. He writes of the crippled stationmaster/porter-in-charge and his wife (who acted as postmistress), the only two (white) inhabitants of Warrina. He writes of flying gangs who worked up and down thirty miles of line, moving camp as required. He describes the two room stone cottages set every ten miles along the line, which served as housing for the twelve men who made up the gang – ganger (in charge) cook and ten navvies. The navvies are not described as any particular background but one ganger at Boorthanna is said to be an old Etonian. The padre gets to travel with the gangers on their section car and evaluate the train line and its bed himself. He also helps out as a volunteer line inspector, saving the ganger from Anna Creek (known as *Balaraung* to the Arabana) some of his sixty mile round trip doing that inspection. By this time there is also a railway doctor, the incumbent being a well-regarded graduate of Guy's Hospital London.

William Creek is described: it is "hardly large enough to deserve the name of township; it consists of the railway station, post-office, residences belonging to each, two other cottages, a tiny school, and a wine-shanty". Aboriginal Australians around are not mentioned. Nowadays it is scarcely larger. Black stockmen get numerous mentions, as do the "black boys" who are everywhere with each white man. But Aboriginal rail workers are not mentioned, even if present, in these books of the 1920s. The padre continues back to Oodnadatta beside the train line, passing Algebuckina train station, with its tremendously long bridge, originally designed to cross the Murray.

Another explorer and geologist, Cecil Thomas Madigan, wrote in 1936 of his travels in Central Australia (separately administered from 1926 to 1931) and found Aboriginal people mainly on pastoral stations. He was pessimistic about the future of Aboriginal people, thinking they may die out or be "preserved" by deliberate isolation. He accepts that 1 in 4 people he met was "half-caste" or similar and that such people were usually acknowledged by their fathers, unlike in many places. Nonetheless, these people were considered Aboriginal by both themselves and the authorities. Madigan, however, did not consider the significance of this. It reflected that underlying the attempt by visitors to the region to paint a bleak picture of Indigenous-settler relations, there was a high degree of both interaction and covert acceptance on all sides.

This sparse literature suggests that Arabana had moved from their original involvement with the train line in the 1880s and 1890s to predominantly a pastoral station life, or a life living beside the train line near ration depots, or still living "myall", an 1835 term meaning Aboriginal Australians not living under settler domination by the time of the First World War, 1914-1918. The subsequent post-War influenza pandemic may have killed up to half of the Arabana population and it was not until the 1920s that there were a larger number of Arabana again. Francis Dunbar Warren's sanctuary Finniss Springs helped renew the people.

1926 To 1929: Travelling North: The Ghan To The North Of Arabana Country

In 1927, however, the Chief Aboriginal Protector, Mr F. Garnett, commented in his Annual Report: "A proclamation has been made concerning the railway now in process of construction from Oodnadatta to Alice Springs, prohibiting aboriginals [sic] not in lawful employment from being within 10 miles east and west of the line... I recently visited Oodnadatta and its neighbourhood, and am convinced that the police officers will find this step helpful in minimising the evils which would result from the camping of aboriginals [sic] along the line of work."

The workers for the extension this time were white people from Australia, England and elsewhere, as well as Asians and, yes, some Aboriginal Australians, many of whom had worked on the Northern Territory line building as far south as Pine Creek from Darwin. The mere fact of wishing to ban Aboriginal Australians is proof that they did live up and down the line. The caveat of "not in lawful employment" also logically means that some Aboriginal Australians were already ongoing workers upon the train line. Aboriginal labour was considered a normal part of extending the line.

This next stage of building between 1926 and 1929 took the railway through another people's country: the Arrernte. It is no accident that Arabana man Reg Dodd's father Alan Buzzacott was southern Arrernte – the railway line linked these peoples in ways scarcely possible before. Obviously there had been prior contact but it was greatly enhanced and accelerated by the train line. For instance, cattle started to be brought by Arrernte drovers to the railway for shipment south, as related by Ted Strehlow in his wonderful 1969 book *Journey to Horseshoe Bend*.

The contract for building the next and final linking section was offered for the ensuing part of the whole line from Oodnadatta to Pine Creek in the Northern Territory on the land grant system at the extraordinary rate of 79,725,000 acres for the 1,063 miles to be built. This works out at 75,000 acres per mile of railway built; about 120 square miles per mile of railway. This would have been through the lands of the Arrernte and half a dozen other tribes. Despite this offer there were no takers and the proposal lapsed with the onset of the Great Depression in 1929. The South Australian Government had in any case bankrupted itself with its huge public works, the Overland Telegraph and the Northern Railway, and the Commonwealth Government was preoccupied with other issues.

Because of the financial struggles, it is not such a surprise that the Northern Territory, controlled by South Australia since 1863 when it was proclaimed as separate from New South Wales by the Imperial Government, had been ceded by the South Australian Government to the Federal Australian Government in 1911. The Federal Government took over control of the Northern Australian Railway completely on 1st January 1926 and it then became called the Commonwealth Railways.

The Second World War from 1939 to 1945 made a major impact on Aboriginal employment. Oodnadatta in 1948 was the site of a visit from the Berndts, who have written about this in *From Black to White in South Australia* in 1951. The railway having moved its railhead to Alice Springs had shrunk the population of Oodnadatta to about 324 people, mostly Aboriginal Australians. The Berndts considered that the main groups were Antakarinja, Pitjatjantjara, and Arrernte. There were three Aboriginal sections to the town: "camps" of usually temporary dwellings of poor quality around the edge of town, some "in-betweens" and a group usually married into the broader community with some accepted social status. Employment was high, as non-Aboriginal people were so few. Rail workers did include day labourers, gangers and fettlers. They comment that this "classification" was not hard and fast: personality made a big difference. A big measles epidemic had scourged the town in 1948 and killed at least 100 Aboriginal Australians, mainly the old and infants. Aboriginal Australians in that area who were not employed by the Commonwealth Railways were paid a lower rate than other workers, and pastoral employers were opposed to equal pay.

Most "Group I", Camp Aboriginal Australians in Oodnadatta knew little English and used "pidgin", just as the Aboriginal negotiator had with Strangways manager John Oastler 100 years before, despite employment. The diet was poor. Gambling took a lot of money. Rations and clothing were issued to aged and infirm by the local constable. "Group II" Aboriginal Australians dressed cleanly, looked after their possessions and had the same diet as non-Aboriginal Australians. "Group III" were very similar to white folk.

Alice Springs, a mere repeater station for the Overland Telegraph before the railway was put through, became a town of 3,000 people by 1962. The Berndts also state that the carrying capacity of the cattle stations increased six-fold due to the availability of transport to move the stock by rail to markets in Adelaide. The Aboriginal Australians from Angas Downs, it would seem, however, did not use the train. They either still walked, or used camels or in some cases were flown, if ill, by the Royal Flying Doctor Service. The use of motor transport by Aboriginal Australians by themselves in that area came after 1962.

There are a number of records by travellers on "the Flash Ghan", the exclusively passenger train, in those days between 1929 and 1980, but the workers are mostly invisible, apart from the iconic train driver and conductor. One conductor told author Derek Whitelock that his wife, upon being told he would be home on Friday, asked, which Friday? A Territorian in the Todd Tavern in Alice Springs told him "it was our lifeline, mate". His Chinese grandfather had worked for 47 years as a fettler and had photographs of the track after a bad flood twisted the line like barbed wire. The English author Michael Frayn recounted to Whitelock the hoary story about a woman who protested the slow progress of the Ghan as she needed to arrive in Alice Springs in time for maternity care. When the conductor retorted that she should not have boarded the train in that condition, she replied that she wasn't in that condition when she had boarded.

There are further uses of the Ghan line recorded. An Aboriginal lady with a sick child was conveyed on the train to the Hospital at Port Augusta. It was not all good, however. When Doris Strangways, an Arabana in her sixties, by then diabetic as so many Aboriginal people have become with western diet, broke her insulin syringe needle on 6th April 1955, the new one was sent by Motorised Section Car on the Ghan line from Alberrie Creek to Curdimurka (47Km). The Railway charged seven pounds, one shilling and five pence for this service!

In the middle of Arabana country, in the twentieth century, Arabana families inhabited the side of the tracks, and hence were involved both in maintaining the line, dealing with emergencies such as derailments as well as taking care of Business, and were on the edges of the line in Marree and Oodnadatta, their lives and stories untold until now. The Aborigines' Protection Board records visiting Marree on 21st September 1955 to select sites to erect houses and washing facilities for Aboriginal Australians in Marree itself. Control was frighteningly micro - even a purchase of three rabbit traps was supposed to be approved by the APB - no wonder the Arabana felt more freedom at F. D. Warren's Finniss Springs Station and working directly for "Charlie Riley", the Commonwealth Railways.

Overall, in summary, the Arabana influenced the route of the old Ghan, worked casually on it for the ensuing fifty years, then became more permanently employed, especially after the Commonwealth takeover. Families lived alongside the line. Many Arabana married non-Arabana men, white, Afghan and Chinese, and their children are considered Arabana. Traditional practices such as ochre pilgrimage parties continued until the First World War, after which the reduced population, cultural change and increasing strictures from Government caused cessation of the practice openly. By the end of the Second World War, Arabana were working fulltime on the Ghan, started living in railway towns such as Marree and Oodnadatta, and were spreading up and down the line to Port Augusta, Alice Springs and even Darwin. The line had not only provided the Arabana with the geographical mobility to move well beyond their country, but the social mobility to secure a foothold in white society.

One of the many historical Rail signs placed at every train stop along the Old Ghan Route.

(Photograph courtesy of Susan SP Dodd)

4

ARABANA ON THE RAILWAY:

"I've Been Working On The Railroad"
(Traditional)

The Early Days Of Steam In Arabana Country

From the very time that the train arrived in Marree in 1884. Aboriginal people carried coal for the trains there. Perhaps they had even done so further south when the train reached Government Gums, (Farina), as they went on their pilgrimages for the sacred red ochre. Knowledge of this phase in history is very limited.

These ochre pilgrimages would have been central in introducing the Arabana to the railways. Philip Jones in his fascinating 2007 book *Ochre and Rust* notes that the substance was conceptualised in many sacred transformations including "emu's blood", *Kurringie Warragurta*, by the local Adnyamathantha tribe who were in charge of the ochre mine 25 Km southwest of Parachilna near the entrance to Brachina Gorge. Another story is that Arabana saw the same ochre as "Dingoes' Blood" after an ancestral hunter had tracked and killed certain dingoes. Jones notes that it was the train line which enabled Aboriginal Australians to travel quickly and safely to the ochre mines and back. It saved them about two weeks' walking either way. The 25-35Kg lumps of ochre could just be put on the train until disembarkation rather than carried on their heads. It also saved them from trigger happy white settlers along the route - they could just sail by on the railway. Indeed, in the very early days, in 1863, there had been an abrupt cessation of ochre pilgrimages for several years when the manager of Beltana Station shot three Aboriginal Australians on their trip towards the ochre mines. The arrival of the railway enabled the pilgrims to bypass this sort of deterrent. Sometimes, however, it seems, it was just to take a ride - they became tourists! Reminiscing in the 1980s, one man recounted that Aboriginal men who had inveigled a free ride from the Marree station-manager by pleading the necessity for more red ochre sometimes then alighted at Commodore siding and then waited for the next train to take them north again, without even venturing into the Ranges.

The Ghan steaming into Oodnadatta 1910
(Photograph courtesy of the State Library of South Australia. SLSA: B 53762)

Jones also comments that the Marree Station Master let ochre parties travel on flat trucks under tarpaulins. They usually got off the train outside the main station at Marree, apparently to avoid attention and also because of the secret nature of the intertribal Mindari ceremonies. The Arabana had their own Wilyaru Ceremony which includes reference to the "Native Cat" or Quoll but, about every two years, participated in an intertribal Mindari ceremony.

Jones seems to interpret the Arabana use of the railway at this time through the constructs of convenience, speed and safety. These ideas are very Western notions and there is an alternative explanation possible. As noted in the previous chapter, the railway followed the Dreaming Tracks necessarily followed by the pilgrims to the ochre mine and hence was permissible and even necessary for the Arabana to travel along. It was a palimpsest, an overlay, to their own Dreaming tracks. Jones affirms that the railway enabled the ochre pilgrimages to continue for at least another generation.

Working For The White Men

There was no Chief Aboriginal Protector from 1856 through to 1908 by direct decision of the colonial South Australian Government. There were Sub-Protectors for the Far North who provided Annual Reports. Protector Field reported in 1901 that Anna Creek pastoral station had 139 people of whom 85 were able bodied Aboriginal Australians, and 20 were constantly employed. Two were reported as dying from scurvy in the previous year, which is quite horrifying when one knows of the vast range of dietary vegetable plants available prior to white settlement which would avert this disease. The nature of the constant employment is tacitly assumed to be pastoral work, but this is not explicit. Oral testimony from my own informants suggests that, at the least, Arabana were providing food through their work on Strangways Springs/Anna Creek to the railway workers and probably day labour in that era. Field also states that there were 113 "Aboriginals" in Oodnadatta the same year, but employment is not mentioned. Field makes specific comment on the large number of "half-castes" living "in the blacks' camp". The Chief Protector was the legal Guardian of all these people, children and adults.

William Garnet South was Chief Protector from 1908 when he

assumed the post until 1922 (with a gap in 1911 and 1912). Originally a policeman, South thought that "full-bloods" would die out and that "half-caste" or even lesser "mixtures" should be separated from their parents. He states in an early annual report that Aboriginal Australians in the Far North were getting wages of 10-15 shillings per week for pastoral work - this was at a time when fettler railway workers got 22 shillings and 6 pence per week. It is unclear, as elsewhere in Australia, whether the pastoral worker Aboriginal Australians ever saw these putative wages. Ronnie Dodd, an Arabana fettler from the 1950s, specifically states that railway wages were the first money he had seen.

By 1919, the Annual Reports state that "the condition of the Aborigines in the Marree district is exceedingly good, there being plenty of employment for the able bodied men who earn good wages at droving and camel driving, the wages being from 4 pounds to 7 pounds a month plus keep". As noted above, it is likely that Arabana were employed on a short term basis by the railways as well. The Influenza pandemic then supervened from 1919 to 1922: nearly half the Aboriginal population up and down the Ghan are reported to have died.

1920s and 1930s

Arabana people were living on pastoral stations, in camps beside railway sidings for instance at Curdimurka, and had moved into Oodnadatta and Marree. Their numbers were increasing once more. Traditional practices had been interrupted, although language and customs had continued. In 1923 the Aborigines (Training for Children) Act was passed which meant that Aboriginal children could be removed from their families against their will and sent to institutions until they were adults. The enactment of former Chief Protector South's vision provided the new Chief Protector with the power to commit any Aboriginal child to an institution and to be detained until they reached the age of eighteen. Because this Act sought to train Indigenous children to be "useful" members of the dominant white society, it further – and intentionally – weakened traditional Aboriginal culture. This assault on Indigenous culture was sustained and the removals of children from their families continued for 40 years under the near total authority of the Chief Protector. Many Arabana children, however, were not removed because of the efforts of pastoralist Francis Dunbar Warren. As his children were considered 'half-castes', and as there was no schooling on Finniss Springs Station until 1939, they were raised according to Arabana culture and able to speak Arabana language. When police, acting on behalf of the Protection Board, tried to remove Warren's children in the 1910s, he evicted them from his earlier Anna Creek property at gunpoint. Consequently, few Arabana, were taken away by the revitalized Aboriginal Protection/Native Welfare. Finniss Springs Station, re-established in 1922, became a haven for Arabana, Dieri and others. It also became a Mission from 1939, with school and church.

Construction of the North-South Railway North-South Railway, April 1928. Scooping up gibbers and earth to make the formation.
(Photograph courtesy of the State Library of South Australia. SLSA: [B 72167/3])

The Commonwealth Government, having assumed control of the railways from 1926, had built an extension from Oodnadatta to Alice Springs between 1926 and 1929. The South Australian Government, allegedly concerned about the negative impact of railway construction workers upon Aborigines, passed a proclamation under Section 33 of the Aborigines' Act prohibiting Aboriginal Australians from being within 10 miles of the train line unless "in lawful employment". Clearly this meant that Aboriginal Australians had been living next to or visiting the train line. Rather than pastoral work or indigence, Aboriginal Australians could work on or get rations directly from the railways. The statute was not effective in Arabana country because the Arabana did provide labour and other services, which was the loophole.

After the Commonwealth Government assumed responsibility for the line in 1926, it offered Aboriginal Australians wage parity with white employees. By 1933, the Chief Protector's Annual Report complains "many refuse employment in *(pastoral)* stations because they want award wages". This is precisely what the Commonwealth Railways were offering. Arabana and others were voting with their feet. With increasing educational opportunities and proximity to the line, Aboriginal groups such as the Arabana and Dieri increasingly sought and secured work on the railways, attracted by the increased freedom and the money. Mr Aiston, Sub-Protector in Dieri country, writes that "a lot to cross over to the Finniss in the Arabunna district" and interestingly "one fairly large party from here have sent me back word they are in the Kingoonya district on the East-West line". That is, both groups were heading to the railways. If the Ghan line did not suffice, the East West line attracted them. Chief Protector W G South repeatedly complained about this from 1922 onwards. Anthropologist Peter Elkin characterised this moving to the proximity of the railway as "intelligent parasitism" in an influential article which this book partly debunks, because work as well as begging occurred. Another author, Gale, wrote in 1964 "In the Northern part of the State the pastoral industry is the only significant employer of labour except the Commonwealth Railways and a few mining enterprises (Leigh Creek and Andamooka). This contrasts sharply with other parts of the State where "most Aborigines are semi - or untrained and are employed only seasonally".

1940s Onwards

During the Second World War trains on the Ghan line increased from two a week to seven a day, a huge jump. Troops, munitions and armaments, not just Australian troops but from other Commonwealth countries and the United States, were using Australia as a base to fight the Japanese. Moving these up to the north and bringing personnel back for rest and recreation, or to recover from wounds meant much higher volumes of traffic. Moreover, labour was at a premium. Women, Italian prisoners of war and Aboriginal Australians were recruited. Arabana stepped up, as happened elsewhere in Australia. Bruce Shaw records ongoing casual mobile employment from the 1940s on the train line for Aboriginal Australians, among others, to fix washaways and continue maintenance. Arthur Ah Chee said that his father (also Arthur) helped many family members become railway workers, including becoming fettlers and gangers. In between such employment the men would drove stock for landholders such as Sidney Kidman.

The trend to employ Arabana on the Ghan accelerated after the War. Their employment marked a shift in the status of the Arabana workers on the line. The War had provided the impetus for advancement both economically and socially for these workers. Many

Indigenous workers were listed in the Commonwealth Railway's records. One of these was Dave Warren – a member of the Arabana Warren dynasty – who commenced work in 1949 as a ganger and stayed with the railways until 1976. He was one of many Arabana, including the Warren family, Arthur (deceased), Stan and Clarrie, who worked on the Ghan, and the stories of the latter two are part of this book.

There was one fascinating instance of how Aboriginal Australians were still regarded when Walter Kidman, son of the "cattle king" Sir Sidney Kidman, wrote to the Chief Civil Engineer, Mr Hannaberry, on 19th March 1946 after the War and said that he wanted "his Aborigines" back to work on pastoral stations such as Macumba. The Railway Commissioner, after due deliberation, wrote back and said that Mr Kidman could have the "Full-Bloods" but they would keep the "Half-Castes", "some of whom have been employed for quite some time". There was still, even after World War II, that sense that Aboriginal Australians were owned by the white pastoralists. This retention and further recruitment of Aboriginal "half-caste" workers was reiterated in a further letter from the Commissioner of 25th August 1960.

The Commonwealth Railway was benefited by recruitment of the Arabana as they lived with their families beside the train line. They did not leave the area except to transact traditional business. Gradually Arabana families moved into Marree, initially on the "wrong side of the tracks" then in the main part of the town. Other prominent families with surnames such as Warren, Dodd, Stuart, Hele and others from Finniss Springs, also found work on the railway. Like many in the region, they gravitated from the pastoral industry to settlements along the line. Indicative of this is the fact that 85 of the 100 residents of Marree were said in 2011 to be Dodd extended family members.

Alan Buzzacott, the father of current Arabana elder Reg Dodd, was recruited as a fettler around 1954. It coincided with the end of Reg's formal education at the age of 14. As was the trend, after working in the pastoral industry at Stuart's Creek Station, Reg Dodd gained work on the railway in 1960, and continued until the line closed completely in 1986.

This was quite unlike "foreigners", also called "aliens", who would mostly come, work for a time then leave. Nonetheless, immigrants and refugees, displaced persons, who came after the War were very much part of the broadening of horizons for their Arabana co-workers.

Arabana men on ochre pilgrimages, continued to travel as passengers on the train to go to Curdimurka to perform Business, that is traditional ceremonies. The intermingling of 20th century capitalism and Aboriginal social practice continued. Michael McKinnon has made a series of six short films about the Arabana called "Marree Arabunna Museum: Six Short Films" (about 2009) and one is called "the railway was good to us". This recounts the work experience of several men from the Dodd family. They were paid real money wages in little yellow envelopes. Like many Arabana rail workers, the railway provided a means for economic and social advancement. One significant career is that of John Hodgson, the uncle of Indigenous academic, Professor Veronica Arbon. He became the first Arabana to qualify as a train driver. Another is Mervyn Dodd, who became the Yardmaster, a highly responsible position, at Port Augusta. The line provided the mobility for the Arabana to advance in the railways and laid the basis by which future generations could contribute to trades and professions well beyond Arabana country.

"The Cold War" Period

> "Where they make a desert they call it peace"
> Tacitus, *Agricola*, 30

The onset of the Cold War of the 1950s and 1960s had a direct and profound impact on the Arabana and their country. After the Second World War, the Australian Government assisted the British Government by testing atomic bombs in the western desert. Over seven hundred nuclear devices were detonated. For instance, on 15th October 1953 Totem One distributed a large radioactive dust cloud eastward over Arabana country. Many Arabana, and other Anangu people, were affected by respiratory and skin complaints and later an increased incidence of cancers. Reg Dodd, for instance, recalls that he was told to stay indoors just by his mother, as there was no warning from the authorities.

In 1961 Aboriginal Australians were officially allowed to vote. After this easing of restrictions, many more Arabana worked on the Commonwealth Railways. One Arabana man, Dudley Barnes, declared to me "the railway was number one for blackfellas". What he as a fettler had to do, he said, was lay nine new sleepers then "sit down the rest of the day and do your own business". "Fresh tucker, clothes" and other goods were sent up on the train from the dedicated stores at Port Augusta and "we lived like kings". Then there was the "tea and sugar" train, carriages with supplies sent up the line, and a butcher's shop also in a wagon. Milk came up on the train and there up to three cars full of stores: "it was like Christmas", chuckled Barnes, "when these arrived". One carriage was also set up as a movie theatre. The railway corridor provided goods and services, and access to the dominant white society and culture which was denied to other Aboriginal peoples not in contact with the line.

Children grew up playing on the railway and its surrounds. Matt and Colleen Strangways, children of Syd Strangways, recall playing in the rail sheds on weekends at Alice Springs in the 1970s. They would enter the locomotive shed and use the gantry as a swing. Holidays were taken by travelling on the train to Marree, Stirling or even holiday houses on the beach at Glenelg which were owned by the railways. The family would go on the goods train which was slow and involved much shunting, and not on the "Flash Ghan" which was reserved for passenger traffic. It would take three days for the goods train to get to Port Augusta from Alice Springs.

Other technological changes were also starting to make inroads on the monopoly of the railways. "Beef roads" and road trains started to replace the railroad. Commercial air services provided a quicker mode of transport between Adelaide and inland towns and settlements. It also allowed a more effective form of healthcare. The Royal Flying Doctor Service started coming directly to Marree from Broken Hill and later from Adelaide. Access to radio and television from 1956 in Australia altered people's knowledge and perceptions of their own country.

The international rise of decolonizing movements and Black Power in the United States also started to make changes in the consciousness of Aboriginal peoples in Australia. The 1939 Cummeragunga Walk-Off, the 1946 pastoral workers' strike in the Pilbara, the 1966 Wave Hill Walk-Off, followed by the 1967 Referendum all increased the power of Aboriginal Australians within their own lands. The referendum result altered the political landscape, paving the way for the recognition of Aboriginal land rights and native title. In 1967, the Gurindji people from Wave Hill pastoral station petitioned the Holt Liberal Coalition Government for the excising of 1295 square kilometres of land from Vesty's pastoral leasehold. This culminated in the handing back of land to the Gurindji people in August 1975 by the Whitlam Government. The 1992 Mabo cases finally allowed recognition of the fiction of *Terra Nullius*. The Wik Determination watered down this Mabo finding but Native Title claims have continued to the present day.

Marree Railhead showing narrow gauge goods shed in background before advent of standard gauge (between 1940 and 1957).
(Photograph courtesy of {http://nla.gov.au/nla.pic-vn4247882})

The End Of The Old Ghan Line
"This Train Is Bound For Glory"

1986 to The Present Day

The Ghan changed to diesel instead of steam engines in 1957. Thus the use of natural springs or bores, derived from the Great Artesian Basin, became unnecessary. That year also, 1957, standard gauge was installed as far as Marree which then became a change of gauge station. For the next eighteen years, Marree became the station where passengers and goods changed to trains fitted for the ensuing narrow gauge stage to Alice Springs. The station at Marree by that time had 25 miles of track in a fairly small area. Nonetheless there were ongoing problems all up the line with floods, washaways, sand blowing over the line and so on, quite apart from the maintenance of all the bridges and culverts associated with the railway. A new Ghan route based on standard gauge started to be laid in April 1975. It started from Tarcoola, a long way west of the old route and out of Arabana country. It is situated 160 kilometres west of the original route, and again ended in Alice Springs. The route was plotted on higher ground than the old Ghan line, to avoid the constant floods that had interrupted the train service. With the opening of the new line, the old one closed down permanently in 1986.

The Ghan as a tourist artefact

The actual tracks and some sleepers from the Old Ghan were torn up and sent to Queensland where new rail lines were being built, mostly for mining. When the Old Ghan closed all the Arabana workers were either forced to move away from their own lands to maintain employment or to stay in their traditional country and seek other work. In Oodnadatta as other railway workers moved away from the town from about 1981 onwards, Aboriginal people leaving the pastoral stations bought the houses and now constitute over half the population.

Reg Dodd opened Arabunna Aboriginal Tours in 1996 and has run this with increasing success. Dodd's business taps into the increasing

Outback tourism market, and the expanding local and international interest in traditional Aboriginal culture. It shows non-Arabana people the extent of the country, some of its former secrets and some of the cultural aspects of traditional and post-contact life. Some of his family also take part in this enterprise such as Esther Kite, his sister and her husband Neville, Vincent, his nephew and others when I did the tour myself.

Some other former rail workers went to Government jobs such as National Parks, Aboriginal Affairs and so on.

The Ghan was extended to Darwin finally in 2004, one hundred years after Federation and more than a hundred and fifty years after South Australia expected the project to link north and south of Australia. This time, however, Social Impact Assessments were prepared and all the Indigenous peoples along the extended new line obtained benefits or compensation. Bruce Chatwin's often maligned book, The *Songlines*, has as the author's guide through central Australia the character Arkady, who is engaged in mediating between surveyors for the Ghan extension and the Aboriginal peoples along the proposed route. This stems from the legal recognition of native title and the passing of land rights' legislation, such as the 1976 *Aboriginal Land Rights (Northern Territory) Act and the 2010 Northern Territory Aboriginal Land Act* which modified access rights to Indigenous lands.

Tourists now drive the Oodnadatta Track, which parallels the old Ghan line for many hundreds of kilometres. The New Ghan train is a luxury rail trip, one of few such in the world, along with The Orient Express, the Trans-Siberian and the Rocky Mountaineer. It has even featured on Chris Tarrant's BBC production, *Extreme Railways*. However, the Arabana's contribution to the line has rarely been celebrated until now.

Oonadatta track and what remains of the narrow gauge Railway heading into Marree township

(Photograph Courtesy of Susan SP Dodd)

The rusting water tank is all what remains of what was Callanna Siding along the Oodnadatta track North of Marree

(Photograph Courtesy of Susan SP Dodd)

5

ARABANA RAIL WORKERS AND THEIR FAMILIES: THEIR STORIES

"Fire and water - they're elementals, aren't they?" Flying Scotsman veteran 2016

This chapter is a series of records of conversations with a number of Arabana railway family members. They are arranged roughly in order of age of informant, ranging from date of birth in 1927 to 1969. They present a vivid picture of life lived on, with and beside the line. The Arabana overwrote some of their Dreaming Tracks with the Railway. They continued to traverse these tracks with the new technology, sometimes with traditional intentions such as visiting family, undertaking pilgrimages, singing the country, trade and so on as well as more western ideas such as moving to a new workplace, "taking holidays" in Port Augusta, learning railway trades and travel just for the pleasure of it.

My own interpolations, where present, are part of the written transcripts supplied to the informants and approved by them.

The ubiquity of the railways for Arabana is a remarkable feature, despite all the other family, geopolitical, micro political and everyday concerns. The patterns of labour, however, bear comment.

A lot of people worked as day labour. Often this was walk-up hiring and people were paid in cash at the end of the day's work. Records are absent or rudimentary. Most people were hired for blocks of two to four weeks at a time for specific tasks such as dealing with floods, washaways and sand-drifts over the line. A significant number, however, were hired on an ongoing basis. I cover each type of labour pattern in the ensuing conversations and interviews, but my contacts, the records and my bias really is towards the more longterm employees. Female informants are fewer in number, although most Arabana men had families and children alongside them on the line. Some women worked as cleaners, laundresses, or in clerical capacities and some examples are given here.

The group of people interviewed are a sample, and by no means all of the workers still living.

The participants' personal stories are from their own perspective, and some persons of whom they speak may be known to them under different names.

Eileen Wani Wingfield, Born 1927

(conversation on 15th March 2012 in Port Augusta)

Eileen (born 1927) is a respected elder who has been keenly involved in anti-uranium protests since the 1980s and has been awarded the Goldman Environmental Prize in 2003. She showed me the actual certificate and her extensive entry in Who's Who 2007.

She said she had three grandmothers, Maggie, Minnie and Jenny. Her mother was Winnie and father Tim Allen, known as Nilpinna Tim (*Nilpinna is a pastoral station 760 Km from Adelaide and about 130Km from Goober Pedy; it is between William Greek and Oodnadatta near Peake Greek, and west of the Oodnadatta Track*).

{*Old Nilpinna mound spring has three main vents, of which two are inside a fenced area of about 5ha. Fencing was done in 1992. The fenced area includes the remains of the Old Nilpinna homestead. The introduced bamboo is predominant at the outlet of the main vent. Three fish species have been recorded at Old Nilpinna. Mature date palms (Phoenix dactylifera) are present at the head of vent 1 (i.e., adjacent to the former homestead)* {Friends of Mound Springs, 2007}.

Her father took her to various areas throughout Country, especially Warrina, Edwards Creek and Mount Margaret. She lived at Mount Barry then the new Mount Margaret Station. She also knew pastoral station manager Archie McLean of Stuart Creek and his son Neil, who grew up with Arabana and spoke the language. She was there a long time. She then went up to Algebuckina. (*All these places are significant Dreaming sites*).

She saw people travelling the "Flash Ghan" (*rapid passenger train*) while mustering cattle. She saw other (Arabana) Elders travelling to Finniss on the railway. Her three grandmothers are buried there at Finniss.

Thereafter she went to Coober Pedy then Mabel Creek then back to Warrina. Back on country she met her first husband and had children. These are Marlene, then she had David and Jennifer.

She considers that she and sister Alma kept the Country alive, especially around Mount Margaret, when others were leaving, going up or down the railway line. Alma lost two children than had five others: Sandra, Raylene, Elaine, Lynette, Charlie and Timothy. Her younger brother Archie Allen was at Finke and kept that Country alive.

She later moved to Port Augusta by train and has lived here since. Some of her children were taken by Welfare: Rebecca *whom I have met*, Joan who has died, Janice whom I have met, Judy, Glen and Winnie. They were returned when they were about aged 18. They had foster parents but were allowed visits every two to three weeks.

Son Glen is now finding lots of evidence at Roxby Downs Uranium Mine about Aboriginal occupation of the area.

Over the past twenty years or more she and others have been fighting the Uranium mining on Arabana and their neighbours' lands. She attributes the Mound Springs drying up to the mine and its profligate use of water from the Great Artesian Basin. She has traveled the world in this pursuit and received the Prize noted above.

There is a sacred Seven Sisters Dreaming women's story of which she is part guardian. She is passing this knowledge on to appropriate people.

She considers she has had a happy life.

This living beside or near the Ghan line and keeping the country alive is considered a vital occupation.

Betty Bowditch, Shirley, Arbon, Zena Richards And Daphne May

(conversation at The Jetty, Darwin, on 13th December 2013).

These ladies are the second, third, seventh and ninth of the children of Charles Dean "Geordie" Hodgson and his Arabana wife Myra Hull. I was introduced by Shirley Arbon's daughter, Professor Veronica Arbon, whom I had originally met in Geelong at Deakin University. We also met (apart from Betty who was in Hospital in Adelaide at the time) very briefly at Finniss Springs in May 2013 then we had this arranged meeting in December. There were apologies from another sister, Lorraine Mills, who lives in Humpty Doo and could not attend. Betty was the eldest attending and said she is older than Syd Strangways, hence his interview appears later!

The Hodgson family minus the oldest sister Marjorie and a brother John who have passed. From left to right in the back row is Maureen, Pamela, Lorraine, Elizabeth, Shirley, Zena and Daphne, Douglas and Gerald in the front row.

(Photograph Courtesy of Professor Veronica Arbon)

Oodnadatta 1926- 1939

Geordie Hodgson was born in the north of the United Kingdom, Tyneside, *(date of birth not given, but probably 1905)* and came to Australia with his brother Alex Hodgson who stayed on in Victoria. Geordie moved to work on the railways, possibly in 1926. Geordie started as a fettler in Oodnadatta, then ganger then later again became a Roadmaster's Clerk, based in Marree and later at Alice Springs. He organised all the picnics for the railway families at Callanna. Geordie died on 2nd July 1966 in Alice Springs.

His wife Myra, Arabana, daughter of Clara (Mudlu) Hull, was born at Anna Creek, or at Coward Springs according to oral tradition, in 1914 and was only sixteen when she legally married. She was nine years junior to Charles. She had thirteen children. She had a hard life but was not removed from her family of origin, unlike sisters Gracie,

Phyllis, and Daisy and some of her brothers. She died in Darwin on 19th August 1965.

Of the thirteen children of Geordie and Myra, Marjorie, the eldest, married non-Arabana man Phil Wallace, who himself was a railway worker. Their son Shane Wallace was a shunter (deceased 1996) and son Adrian a train driver. Adrian lives and works at Roxby Downs Uranium Mine. Marjorie and Phil's daughter Michelle Cooper and another sister Maree live in Port Augusta.

I touch on the second and third children, Elizabeth (Betty) and Shirley below.

The fourth child of Myra and Geordie, Douglas was a jockey, cited in *Aborigines and 'The Sport of Kings'* by John Maynard. He has two daughters and three sons all living in Adelaide.

Pamela, number five, was not discussed. Her married name was Pamela Anne Pension.

The sixth child was John Charles Adrian Hodgson (dob 24/2/43; died 23/6/79) who was a train driver. (*Qualifications confirmed by reference to National Australian Archives personnel file*). He trained at Port Augusta and Darwin but worked mainly on the Darwin to Larrimah line. I have met his son Charlie who is in Alice Springs and whom I have interviewed (see below).

The eldest three surviving children of Geordie and Myra were registered in the AIM Hospital in Oodnadatta. Maureen was born in Port Augusta, Daphne and John in Marree, Lorraine in Hawker and Gerald, the youngest, in Alice Springs.

They were very poor, despite the regular wage from the railways, and it was a very hard life for Myra. Clothes were made from flour bags. Nonetheless they all considered that the train was a vital part of their lives. They got free travel. They would go on the train on holidays to Coward Springs (where Auntie Evelyn was the publican's wife), to Curdimurka for various celebrations or Marree to visit relations or back to Oodnadatta similarly once living in Marree. They visited Quorn, Port Augusta and Stirling North to stay with sister Marjorie and brother Douglas.

Myra at Oodnadatta

(Photograph Courtesy of Professor Veronica Arbon)

Auntie Evelyn and Sid had one son, Frank Churches. Betty remembers him visiting Marree while in Army uniform in 1946. His whereabouts are currently unknown.

Granny Clara often traveled on the Ghan regularly to Finniss Springs, Oodnadatta, Marree, Finke, Port Augusta, Coward Springs and Alice Springs. She visited them in Alice Springs when they were young women, in later years, the 1950s or 1960s.

Marree 1939- 1948

Betty was born 2nd July 1932. The family left Oodnadatta when Betty was aged 7 and moved to Marree. They all lived in a railway house next to the train line. When the War was on, there were many troops travelling through Marree mainly going north. They would hand out some of their rations to the Hodgsons. On the down side the soldiers would steal chickens at night!

Dad was very worried about the War's impact on his family of origin in England. I was given copies of two letters written by Geordie to his family, identified as Beatrice and Joe. The earlier, dated 22nd October 1940, from Marree, expresses patriotic concerns and family concerns. He also mentions another male child who had died by 1940. Two male babies died shortly after birth, hence the total of thirteen born to Myra. In the other letter of 11th September 1941, he does say that Douglas is very energetic and that Myra is well. He longed to go back to visit people in England but the family say this never happened due to cost of airfares. He died before retirement.

Betty was sent to Adelaide to go to school at St Dominic's Priory in North Adelaide, for four years and travelled to and fro on the old steam engine train. She enjoyed holidays coming home to her family and to the other places mentioned above. She also talked of the ability the family had to order goods from the Railway Stores in Port Augusta. It was easier then than now to obtain goods along the old Ghan line, and Railway families were especially favoured. Meat was sent to them from Alice Springs and tinned foodstuffs from Port Augusta.

Shirley Arbon (dob 4/2/1934) attended school in Marree. She remembers Dougie swinging on the train couplings as the train was moving out of the station. Shirley married Raymond and they had seven children. They moved around between the Territory and Queensland.

Zena (dob 23/2/42 in Marree) married Colin Richards and has four children, all born in Darwin.

Maureen Valerie was born on 5th January 1945 in Port Augusta, married Steven Clark and was not further discussed.

Daphne May (dob 5/6/46, born in Marree) married Samuel and has two children.

Lorraine was born in Hawker on 2nd May 1947. She married Francis Mills.

Gerald, the youngest, was born on 25th February 1950 in Alice Springs but was not further discussed, although it was noted he lives in Darwin.

Marjorie, Elizabeth and Shirley Hodgson
(Photograph Courtesy of Professor Veronica Arbon)

Alice Springs 1948 - End Of Childhood

By late 1948 the Hodgson family was in Alice Springs. All cried on leaving Marree. They moved by travelling in the Guard's van on the Ghan. Dust storms in the Alice were very bad, and their house had to be swept out of all the sand that had accumulated. From Alice Springs, Geordie wrote to the Aborigines Protection Board via Mr

Pearce (probably the missionary at Finniss) on 14th June 1948. He asked for dispensation to allow Myra's sisters, Grace and Millie Hull, to come to Alice Springs to be with and look after his wife, who had severe rheumatoid arthritis. This request was denied in a return letter of 1st July 1948, no reason being given.

For Maureen, Daphne and Lorraine, the Railway yard in Alice Springs was their youthful playground. They would rush to meet the Ghan on its arrival. They would play in the loco shed where the trains were kept and raid the tucker box for biscuits. Nearby was a water tank near the loco shed which all the Railway kids used as their swimming pool. The Ghan and the cattle trains "were very long and we had to jump over the couplings to be able to get to school. It wasn't very nice doing that with the cattle trains because the cattle would get restless and move around a lot".

All the sisters regretted not being able to learn Arabana language. Their mother spoke it but their Dad would not allow her to teach the children. Mum could not read or write. When Child Endowment came in during the 1940s, she was taught to sign her name so she did not have to use a thumbprint.

Syd Strangways: "Me And The Railways"

(an annotated typescript, with conversation held in Alice Springs, Friday March 9th 2012).

Syd was born on 15th July 1932 and turned 80 in July 2012. He kindly wrote this set of recollections for this project, and then we discussed the text at the Oasis Hotel over coffee in a private room. He remains a spirited member of the Arabana Aboriginal Corporation and gave the Arabana oration at the May 2013 restoration of the name of Lake Eyre as Kati Thanda.

Syd's father Henry (Wapili) Strangways was born in 1881, son of Lily and Rang (Baguwida) Strangways. His mother Edie (Edith) Sargent (born 1902) was from Horseshoe Bend but had been taken when young and placed in Adelaide to work for a white family. Syd was the second youngest of seven. I have interviewed Wilfred, son of Syd's elder brother Bert (Herbert) Strangways and this conversation appears later.

Although known as a cook upon Finniss Springs, Henry's work upon the railways is not known for certain.

"I was born on and grew up on a property (*Finniss Springs*) that ran both sheep and cattle. All I ever knew from birth was the life of a stockman. And like every other Arabana who grew up on Finniss Springs Mission, I was very good at it.

"I joined the Railways by accident, I guess. A friend of mine, a relative actually, had an agreement with the manager of Cordillo Downs, just up over the order of South Australia and Queensland to break in a large mob of horses in the New Year. He asked me if I was interested in going up and giving him a hand. It was Christmas time and we were in Finniss Springs Mission. Dead broke. Both without a job. We came up with the idea of getting a job with the Railways for a few weeks to get some money so we could catch the Mail Truck up to Cordillo Downs. So we go into Marree and front up to the Roadmaster's (*Joe Kelly*) office and sign up. The requirement then was to go down to Port Augusta to pass a medical examination before being assigned to a fettlers' camp somewhere along the narrow gauge line to Alice Springs. We were both issued with free passes. However, on the night that we were both to catch the slow mixed train down to Pt Augusta, I went to a party and got so drunk that I missed the train completely. Clem (*Dodd*) went, of course. On his own.

"A couple of days after, when I had sobered up, I fronted up to the Roadmaster's office in Marree and they gave me a pass with the instructions to go to Leigh Creek to do my medical and then proceed to the fettlers' camp at Curdimurka. On this instance, I did what was asked of me, and having passed the medical, duly turned up at Curdimurka to start work. This suited me as I knew the area around Curdimurka fairly well. *(Syd had spent time there as a child with his grandmother Lily)*. There were two gangs at Curdimurka at the time. One looked after twenty five miles of track to the north and the other looked after twenty five miles to the south. The bonus for me was that the men in charge of the gangs, as gangers, were both Arabana. Lenny Stuart was the ganger for the northern gang and his father, Laurie, was the ganger of the southern gang. I joined Lenny Stuart's gang on the northern section which suited me as this section included Coward Springs where we could get the occasional carton of beer. In those days it was big bottles in a box of a dozen. Coward Springs had been a famous pub in days gone by but its licence had expired *(the hotel closed completely in 1962)*. Roy Lewitzki, a noted outback character, was there at that time and we had an understanding with him. Roy was an expert leather worker and saddler and was a son in law to the famous Kidman manager of Anna Creek, Archie McLean, a very well-known bushman. Roy Lewitzki was a very old man at that time.

"Meanwhile, Clem had gone to Pt Augusta alright as intended but had got romantically entangled with a local girl and had forgotten about his medical. He was a good looking lad, my mate. Worse still, after a short while, he dumped the local girl for a pretty young lady who was visiting Pt Augusta from Silverton, west of Broken Hill in New South Wales. The upshot of it all was that when she went home, Clem also followed. Not to worry, I thought when I heard about it all, I will work here for a fortnight or maybe a month then collect my pay, follow him over to Silverton and maybe then we could still go on that horse breaking contract. Unfortunately things didn't work out that way.

"I had only been working as a fettler for little more than a fortnight when I got the grim news. Clem had taken on a job at Silverton, a job that he loved and that is breaking in horses. Clem was a reputable rider, as good as any I've seen, and he was an outstanding horseman. The stockyards that he had been working in was made from lengths of discarded railway line. He was riding the horse that had been handling in that yard when it somehow suddenly reared up, slipped and fell causing Clem to hit his head heavily against the railing as horse and rider came down. That fall was fatal. The news when I heard it sickened me and I felt great loss. It also placed me at the crossroads. I could not go up to Cordillo Downs and take on the horse breaking job as the contract was in his name. So I said to myself, what the heck, I'll stay on in the Railways for a while and see what I could do with myself later on. Little did I know that 'later on' would stretch into forty years or more.

Syd Strangways: from Syd himsel with permission

"Curdimurka was not the first time I was employed by the Commonwealth Railways. I don't know what year it was but it rained and rained and there were floods and volumes of water everywhere. The railways were badly affected by flooding and washaways and at a place called Canterberry Creek alone, the floods had washed away almost a mile of track and it ended up a mess of tangled and twisted metal and broken sleepers (*possibly 1946*). The Commonwealth Railways sent out an urgent call for manpower in all directions for help in repairing the damages to the line. Finniss Springs Mission was close by so they desperately asked for men to come and help. I was still going to school then. Six or seven men volunteered to go and, I don't know how, it must have been school holiday time. but I also went along. (Others included Percy Dodd, Alan Buzzacott, Norman Woods and a couple of Warrens possibly Lennie and Roy). We all joined up at Alberrie Creek which was our nearest Railway siding. After a couple of days working on washaways and washouts to the north and south of Alberrie Creek, we were shifted to the big one at Canterberry Creek. The Railways set up a big camp an Wangianna Siding which was about ten miles from the site. A large team of about forty of fifty men set about the task of repairing the track. A completely new bed had to be prepared for the permanent way and new rails and new sleepers put in for a mile or so. It was hard work and mostly was done by pick and shovel.

"I was here when I met my first 'New Australian'. I have never met or seen any foreign men before, not even Germans or Italians. Of course, I had heard of them ... like in school and such. Most of the foreign men who worked there came out to Australia from the Baltic States in Europe and were referred to as 'Balts'. It took us the best part of a fortnight to repair the track enough to let a train pass over. The bloke in charge then brought us back to Alberrie Creek by section car and we walked back into Finniss Springs from there. A few weeks after, we had to go into Alberrie Creek again to meet the slow mixed train (the Chaser) that ran weekly to Alice Springs and which was also the pay train to collect our pay. We all felt like as if we were millionaires!

"I spent about three or four years at Curdimurka in which time I managed to buy a second hand short wheel base Landrover and we used to go everywhere in that. I got promoted to ganger and was transferred to Wangianna to start up the gang there as the previous one had elapsed. On weekends, we used to go back to Finniss Springs. At that time, most people were starting to drift away and move into towns like Marree or Pt Augusta (*mid to late 1950s; Finniss closed completely in 1958*). Then in early 1964 I got itchy feet and put in for a transfer to Alice Springs. After initial opposition from my Roadmaster and Engineer-in-Charge, I finally got permission from the Chief Engineer for a transfer to the gang in Alice Springs yard.

"I arrived in Alice Springs on the 16th of May 1964. There were only about five thousand people in the Alice in them days and everybody knew everybody and it was a real friendly place. As I was a fully qualified ganger and had my papers and qualifications, the Railways were reluctant to leave me as a fettler in the Alice Springs yard gang. It was not long before I was moving up and down the line working at various places and locations as a trouble shooter and as a stand in for other gangers. So I was away from the Alice quite a bit working on different sections of track that were a concern to the powers that be on Pt Augusta and working out problems with staff and personnel. Of course, there were Roadmasters who generally supervised all this but they did not do any actual physical work. I was stationed at Rodinga for a while when I again decided on a change of scenery so I put in for a transfer to the Mechanical Branch as this would then leave me permanently in Alice Springs. I was then with the Civil Engineering Branch. My application, however, was refused so I had a little argument with my engineer-in-charge. Stuff this, I thought, so I came into the Alice and applied for a job at the loco sheds, which at that time had employed just under a hundred men. I went back to Rodinga and put in my fortnight's notice after which I came back into town and started work in the loco sheds as a lifter's (wagon fitter) offsider.

"All this was in the old Commonwealth Railways days. There were principally three main departments. The Civil Engineering department, the Mechanical Engineering department and the Transport Section. The heads of the departments were all responsible to the Commonwealth Railways Commissioner. Everything ran fairly well and the Railways, as a whole, was like a big family. (Workers and bosses were on Christian name basis).

"I progressed from being an offsider to be a fully qualified lifter and worked at that for a while. I had another change in job description when I was successful in my application for a vacant position of wagon painter. Most rolling stock and wagons had to be repaired, repainted and re-lettered every three years or so. Mostly all rolling stock was painted in the colour red with white letters and numbers. I worked at that for a time but found it was a dirty messy kind of job so when the position of train lighting examiner became vacant, I put in an application for it. The Train Lighting Examiner was responsible for all lighting in brakevans and carriages and this included the carriages on the passenger train, the Ghan. The Ghan, of course, always had a power van attached which generated power throughout the train but the brakevans and carriages on slow and mixed goods trains and other trains relied on a bank of twelve two volt batteries, carried on the carriage itself, for lighting and power. It was up to the train lighting examiner to maintain these and keep them in good working order to provide lighting and power. I worked at the train lighting job for some time before moving back to the loco sheds to work again as a Lifter (wagon fitter). It was hard work and noisy, I guess. My mates and colleagues gave me the nickname of 'Banga' because I was always banging on about something. It was a take, I think, from my surname, Strangways, as they also sometimes called me 'Stranga'.

"During my time working there the Railways changed its name from the Commonwealth railways and formed itself into a Commission and called itself the Australian National (*1st July 1975*). To many of the old workers and people around, the Commonwealth Railways was referred to as 'Charlie Riley' and it was not uncommon to hear old railway people say 'I am working for Charlie Riley'. As the Commonwealth Railways, the railway was heavily subsidised by the Australian Government. As a commission, it started to make its own way and began to make a profit in its own right. In the late 1980s or the early 1990s, when everything seemed to be going well, the powers that be down south (the Commonwealth Government, I think) decided in their wisdom to privatise the Railways and sold it off to private concerns (Gave it away free, some people said).

A lot of the old railway men, in disgust, left in great numbers and the new owners were forced to hire and recruit new personnel. A lot of us were offered redundancy packages and I left the services of the Railways in 1994. Pretty sad day, really. A few of the men who were made redundant signed up again with the new owners who called themselves the National Railways. But life in the service of the Railways was never the same again. It had lost its feel of identity".

Syd said to me in October 2014 that the down side of railways was the introduction of diseases such as the post-World War I pandemic of Influenza which killed many Arabana living near the train line.

Official statistics recount that 10,000 people died in Australia as a result of this illness but many Aborigines' deaths were not notified to the authorities. (Barry, 2009; Basedow in his 1920 visit did note the depopulation due to this pandemic).

Clarrie Warren

(a conversation held at Oodnadatta on 24th June 2103)

Clarrie (or Clary) was born at Finniss Springs in 1936 to Arthur Warren (born 10th May 1910; died 1989; himself the eldest son of Francis Dunbar Warren and Laura Baralda) and Rosa Murray (Dieri people). Arthur himself worked on the railway line and was interviewed by Bruce Shaw, appearing in the book "*Our Heart is the Land*" (1995). Clarrie had five sisters and two brothers. Brothers Max (Francis Maxwell) and Ross both worked on the railway (Ross' interview is elsewhere recorded). Sister Jennifer also worked on the railway, but her capacity was not stated.

Clarrie was reared at Finniss Springs where he attended the Mission school of some 46 Aboriginal children run by Andrew Pearce. Francis Dunbar Warren, his grandfather, taught him to drive a vehicle. At the age of 13 in 1949 he became a stockman working at Witchelina.

In 1956 he joined the Commonwealth Railways as a fettler in Farina. His uncle Dave Warren, who worked for the railways for 36 years, was his first ganger. Clarrie considers that Dave taught him everything he knows. There were six or sometimes eight in a gang and they inspected the line from Farina to Copley three times a week. If there were no defects there was still regular maintenance to be carried out. The remains of Clarrie's house are still to be seen in Farina. Clarrie was involved in the change to standard gauge which reached Marree in 1957. This went all the way from Port Augusta to Marree which remained a change of gauge station, becoming narrow gauge from there to Alice Springs. Clarrie had time off with sickness and for family reasons. He returned to the Commonwealth Railways at Curdimurka at the age of 23. His house there was lit by Tilley lamps, had a kero frig and a donkey (wood-fired boiler) for hot water. Other fettlers from many nations were his friends. Pastoral station owners supplied meat to the fettlers and in return the railway men used to help out on the stations on weekends.

Typical settlers cottages on northern railway. Hergott to Oodnadatta, May 1928 (Photograph Courtesy of the State Library of South Australia [B 11733])

Clarrie has also worked at Alberga, Abminga and elsewhere. He became a relief ganger and worked at Coward Springs. When his children were young he moved to Port Augusta for their education and continued on the Old Ghan railway working all the way from Copley to Alice Springs.

Two of his sons worked on the railway too, one in a special gang re-sleepering the line.

In about 1976 Clarrie married Audrey Stewart (Macumba area) and he has lived at Oodnadatta for many years.

He was the last Aboriginal ganger in Oodnadatta when the Old Ghan closed. He retired rather than move to the New Ghan.

Clarrie says that grandfather Francis Dunbar Warren's brother George Warren was involved in surveying for the old Ghan line.

(Ian Morison in *The Warrens* {2012} gives the following: George Warren, Francis Dunbar Warren's uncle, born 21/9/1820, was trained as a surveyor, graduating in 1841. He apparently surveyed for the route of one of the first railways in Scotland. After 1848 work on local Springfield matters had been completed in South Australia and George was able to concentrate on other survey work further north. Afghans and Arabana were involved with him during these years. George died on 26/2/1895 two days after a train accident, trying to cross the line in a buggy in front of the locomotive. Morison is silent on George's work with regard to the Old Ghan survey. There was a second George Warren, but he was only 19, albeit at Anna Creek, by the time the Old Ghan line was completed to Oodnadatta).

Kevin Buzzacott

(conversation on 23rd March 2012. Also present were Julian {undertaking video recording} and Edward Cranswick, whose house we met in).

Kevin Buzzacott is a respected Arabana elder and political activist. He is fighting against the Roxby Downs Uranium mine and its expansion. Edward Cranswick, a "white" man, through his Hogarth forebears, is related to Kevin.

Kevin started by asserting that "we are in a war", but then moved to a more general discussion.

His ancestors, the old people, met "explorers", then Afghans, then Telegraph workers, settlers and so on. The explorers had reported great land for the picking (the concept of *terra nullius* at that time) and the settlers followed. Grandfather Francis Dunbar Warren took up Finniss Springs in 1906. He took Aboriginal people onto Finniss, not only Arabana but lots of others. These included Dieri, Arrernte and others. In the end the Government wanted him to take over their role with other Aborigines and Warren refused. It was too much. There were over 300 Aboriginal people on or about Finniss Springs. A number of Arabana now live in places like Port Augusta, Coober Pedy, Oodnadatta and Alice Springs.

As the settlers moved north (from the 1860s), they established "way stations" or rolling depots, like bridgeheads into foreign country: Hawker, Farina, Beltana then onto Marree. Narrow gauge railway was the means of such way stations being supplied. Towns grew up from these sites.

Kevin Buzzacott 2007
(Photograph Courtesy of Susan SP Dodd)

Arabana worked for pastoralists and this enabled the people to stay on country. That was the good side. Aboriginal stockmen were mainly paid in clothes and rations. But there was the down side of the arrival of the pastoralists and the train too. Dispossession occurred, as later people were put off the land for the stock and later miners, and then there has been the misuse of the railway to carry Uranium. As far back as Boer War days (*1899-1902*), however, Arabana would jump the train and travel up and down to get a job.

The Oodnadatta extension line (completed in 1891) was delayed because rails were brought out from England by ship. The Algebuckina Bridge was designed to cross the Murray River but was put over this river instead.

Francis Dunbar Warren supplied Aboriginal stockmen for musters on other stations, for shearing and then from about the 1940s, men to work on the railways. There had been railway work in the Great Depression (*1929 to mid 1930s*). Up and down the line now known as Pichi Richi, Chinese workers had been used, especially for stonework at which they were expert. In the 1940s there was a big washaway north of Marree, with about 2 miles of track washed away; the steel tracks were bent around trees like liquorice. Sleepers were gone. The Railways rang Francis Dunbar Warren because they needed workers immediately. Lots of Arabana men went including Alan Buzzacott, Kevin's father. As they were good workers, the Commonwealth Railways kept them on. By then there was quite some competition for Aboriginal workers as a desired hard-working labour force.

Alan Buzzacott and his family stayed with the railway for more than 20 years and settled in Marree. In time off work, the families could catch up with each other. Pay was equal – unusually for the time - and reasonable. They initially stayed in fringe camps, then as houses became available, they moved into the railway houses. Some still exist and are used today. Some have been bought and sent elsewhere.

Arabana fettlers on destroyed bridge

Arabana became gangers, foremen and so forth, and virtually ran Marree. In World War 2, fettlers were involved in civil defence. Flat tops were fitted with sandbags, as were the stations, and the men issued with 303 rifles. The fettlers, including Alan Buzzacott and other uncles and brothers in law, rode the line between Alice Springs and Marree on these flat tops in case the Japanese came. As a child, Kevin used to play with discarded cartridge cases, an old machine gun and similar detritus of war. Shell cases would be used as toy cars.

Kevin was present as a child when the standard gauge came to Marree in 1957. He can be seen in a photograph with various uncles published in the newspaper of the day with the dignitaries (including Sir Arthur Fadden, Acting Prime Minister and Sir Thomas Playford, SA Premier).

Kevin worked for the Railways on and off for many years. Rails increased in size and weight from 20Kg to 90Kg to carry heavier and heavier loads, up to 40 tonnes. There were fettlers' camps each 15 to 25 miles. Some camps were mobile and some were standing camps. They dealt with buckled track, washaways, derailments, sand covering the track and so on. It was hard work in heat and cold. Bosses could be like slavedrivers. Coal fallen from the old steam trains tenders was picked up by the fettlers and other Arabana to use as fuel for their fires. There were dams and tanks, as many fettlers' camps had no natural water supply. One of Kevin's jobs was to pump water into the tanks.

Once, at William Creek, there was a derailment and food supplies for the 150 passengers of the Ghan were running short. Kevin carted food in old tea chests packed with ice, pulled along on a section car. It took half one day and half a night and was a slog until he pulled up about midnight. Then he and his colleagues worked overnight to repair the track itself. There was no overtime then!

He also worked on a derailment just north of Algebuckinia where fifteen trucks jumped the track. It was very hot and they had to rebuild the line. Sometimes spur lines were put in while the original tangle was sorted out.

Kevin was there when the piggyback trains came in (after the change of gauge in 1957). They had to stop the engines to do the transfers. He thinks that the locomotives were Swiss and sleepers came originally from the United Kingdom, then Western Australia, but local timber was used if none other available.

Kevin was a ganger at Tarcoola and encouraged his Aboriginal colleagues to study hard, including a man who stayed on with the current private rail company and become a boss.

After the Ghan line closed (in 1983), the rails were sent to Queensland for creating train lines to transport the sugar. The Leigh Creek coal mine train line still ran. He and some colleagues originally wanted to keep a section between Marree and Curdimurka open for tourism, movies etc, but this did not happen.

Nowadays Kevin is fighting for return of Arabana land. He says that the old people have been buried in many places around country and they need their respect. The Mound Springs will not recover for over twenty years due to the volume of water being taken by the Uranium miners to process their mineral. Other sacred sites have been destroyed due to the putting through of roads for the mines. There are a number of burials up and down the line also as workers were just buried where they dropped.

Kevin is suing BHP Billiton and the Federal Minister responsible for this desecration. Fukushima was a wake-up call.

Reg Dodd

(conversation 15/6/2013 And Other Talks In Marree)

Reg Dodd was born in 1940 on Finniss Springs Station to Tom Dodd and Amy Warren, daughter of Francis Dunbar Warren (born 1878) by his Arabana wife, Laura Baralda. Reg was schooled to age 14 at the Mission School on the Station. Finniss Springs, unlike other pastoral stations, had birth certificates for each Aboriginal person born there, there were bank accounts and bank books for Aboriginal workers, and the Flying Doctor Service used to specifically visit that Station.

Reg is sure that his Arabana great grandfather, Laura Baralda's father, together with Francis Dunbar Warren, persuaded Aboriginal men not to attack an Overland Telegraph construction camp. The Arabana men had been coming for a sacred ceremony around "Hermit Hill", also known as Pregnant Woman or *Bullaburra*. The construction camp had been sited about 800 metres from this "St Paul's Cathedral". They also persuaded the men to move the ceremony to a more secret and private place near Curdimurka. Thus massacres and reprisals did not occur in Arabana country unlike, say, in Dieri lands.

Reg after leaving school worked on Anna Creek Station for several years from about 1954. His stepfather, Allan Buzzacott, had got an ongoing job on the railways in 1954, hired by Roadmaster Des Dunning. Reg then joined the Commonwealth Railways, initially as a fettler, but later promoted to Train Examiner. Reg was on the railways for 26 years altogether, including after the Ghan ceased to run on this old line, through to February 1987.

In the 1980s, linguist Luise Hercus and anthropologist Ted Strehlow involved Allan Buzzacott, who was Southern Arrernte, in their research on Aboriginal people. Reg went with Luise Hercus to Hamilton Station, to the old people's camp, where, to the anthropologists' surprise, Reg was greeted as a known person. This Station is 100Km north of Oodnadatta and 135Km south of Aputula/Finke.

Reg was part owner of Finniss Springs Station, which had been left by Francis Dunbar Warren to his Aboriginal family. His mothers Flora and Amy had fought to keep the Station but this lapsed about 1978. He started the Marree Arabunna People's Committee. He worked with Environment and Planning. Reg worked with South Australian Aboriginal Heritage. He was a key informant for Jen Gibson and Bruce Shaw. He now continues to run Arabunna Aboriginal Tours. He has been involved with Pembroke College in Adelaide from 1995. His own grandchildren from daughter Jackie and Ronnie Dadleh, Kyle and Curtley, have been to Trinity College in Melbourne. His son, Terrence, known as Kootchi, works for Centrelink.

Reg has strong traditional links all up and down the old Ghan line, for instance to the Doolans at Aputula, the old Finke. He is connected to Audrey Stewart, a custodian for the Macumba, now living in Oodnadatta (see interview). This set of connections via the railway is a palimpsest of the older story or songlines which run all the way from Port Augusta to the Tiwi Islands.

Arabana Railworkers

Reg sees the railway as part of a transitional mechanism for Arabana people to move from hunter gatherers to join modern economic society. It was different to pastoral ways, as money was used as a reward, rather than goods or rations. Pastoralism had some advantages in that quite personal relationships were set up between Aboriginal people and white people: He cited Frank Booth, the mailman from about 1900 to 1920, who had an Aboriginal wife. He recalled Tom Kruse, the famous mailman and his Aboriginal partner Henry Butler, who appears in a 1954 video clip and is named in Kristin Weidenbach's biography of Kruse, *Mailman of the Birdsville Track* (p101-2). Archie Maclean from Peake Station worked closely with Reg's uncle, Arthur Warren, and learned Arabana himself.

But regular wages, equal to those of other workers from non-Aboriginal backgrounds, were a novelty for Arabana and other Aboriginal pastoral workers. Thus the Commonwealth Railways, which paid such equal wages from the time they took over the Great Northern Railway, the Ghan, from 1927 onwards, was a significantly different employer.

Ross Warren

(interview on 1/7/2013 at his home in Bendigo, in the company of Lyn, his wife).

Ross was born at Finniss Springs in 1941 to Arthur Warren (died 1989; himself the son of Francis Dunbar Warren and Laura Baralda) and Rosa Murray (Dieri people). There were four sisters and two brothers: Francis Maxwell, Francis Clary (or Clarrie), Gloria (Colson), Ross himself, Betty and Peggy (both Larkins), and Jennifer. Brothers Max (Francis Maxwell) and Clarrie both worked on the railway and I interviewed Clarrie in Oodnadatta (see above).

Ross was recruited to the Railways at Marree on 8th September 1960 aged 19. He went initially to Port Augusta then Curdimurka where he worked as a fettler. There were about 10-14 men there and they worked putting in new steel rails and wooden sleepers on the narrow gauge which still ran from Marree to Alice Springs. Concrete sleepers were tried between Beresford and Coward Springs but were not successful at that time.

They had very little machinery and work was done by heavy manual labour.

By the time Ross was at Curdimurka no traditional activities were occurring there, he says.

He was at Curdimurka for about 2-3 years and then at Wangianna with Syd Strangways as ganger.

Subsequent postings included: Nullarbor, Barton, Tarcoola, Ooldea, O'Malley and Hughes, Cook, Kingoonya, back to Barton on the Special Gang, Winanowie, Port Augusta then Tent Hill, Brachina, Farina, Stirling North, Wilktana, Nevrolda, Mingary, Manna Hill, Yunta, Cockburn, Peterborough, Crystal Brook, Balaclava, Gawler and Barossa Valley.

He finished in 1993 after 33 years on the Railways. He then came to Bendigo where he now lives with Lyn, his wife. (Lyn says that she is Stolen Generations herself, discovering her heritage in her forties. She is Yorta Yorta/Wemba Wemba and a cousin is my former boss Lance James at the Victorian Aboriginal Health Service. She is the great niece of both Granny Geraldine Briggs and Marj Tucker).

He enjoyed his life on the Railways, meeting people, seeing a lot of the country. He had many international co-workers.

Achievements he is proud of include breaking the American speed record for putting in concrete sleepers from Port Pirie to Crystal Brook.

He recalls the excellent range of goods available through the Commonwealth railway shops at Port Augusta, Stirling North, Tarcoola, Cook and Rawlinna. He recalls theatre (cinema) on a monthly basis in a special carriage on the train. He recalls bringing sick kids by Section Car to medical aid. He recollects finding green tektites from meteorite impacts on the Nullarbor.

He has a daughter Lyn who is married to Lionel Milera (Arabana), one grand-daughter, one grandson and two great grandchildren.

Martha, nee Dodd, Watts

(interview at her home in northern Adelaide, 26th July 2014) Martha was born on 11th December 1943 at Broken Hill, eldest child of the six children of Percy ("Nobby") Dodd and Sheila Strangways, both Arabana. Martha's other siblings were Mervyn, Leon Michael, Rhonda, Lionel (also interviewed for this book) and Theresa.

Percy was one of the sons of Amy, daughter of Laura Beralda, and Tom Dodd. Percy's wife, Sheila, was a daughter of Henry (Wapili) Strangways, Arabana, and Edie (Edith) Sargent, Arrernte.

After a rural childhood, including schooling at the Mission school on Finniss itself, Martha was kidnapped from Finniss aged 13 or 14 and flown by Royal Flying Doctor Service aeroplane to Broken Hill. This move makes her one of the Stolen Generations. From Broken Hill she was sent by train to Sydney then Lake Macquarie. She was placed with a family who put her in a shed out the back. Martha says this family "did not even speak proper English that I could understand. It was very upsetting for one as young as I was at the time".

Later she was sent to six further homes around Adelaide, all private families. She was not allowed to mix with other Aboriginal people, but did so covertly. Even getting to school was discriminatory: she attended the same school as a Minister's two daughters but had to catch a different bus. She was kept under curfew even when other white children in the household were not.

She ran away several times, using Government pocket money. She was released or escaped for the last time in 1959 aged 16 and got home to Marree from Adelaide via the Mixed Goods Train. She managed to get back with joy and relief to her family. Meanwhile Finniss Springs had become non-viable and the families had mostly moved into Marree.

Martha then worked in the Marree Hotel as waitress and cleaner. Thereafter aged about 18 she joined the Commonwealth Railways as a carriage cleaner. She did the first class carriages. After the trip from Alice Springs the carriages were full of fine red sand. She would sweep, mop, varnish the walls of the compartments and Brasso the taps. She would make 130 beds in one shift. She had to lug the mop and bucket, full of the cleaning water, all the way from the loco shed via the transhipping area. Martha also got up at 5am to clean the Budd Car from Port Augusta as well as cleaning the Ghan.

Martha Watts (nee Dodd)
(Photograph Courtesy of Martha Watts)

There were a few women in the cleaning team, some Arabana men and some Afghans. Other names she recalled were Betty Bowditch (Arabana, interview above), Jean (surname not recalled) and Margaret Bejah (Aghan).

With her first pay from the Commonwealth Railways she bought a transistor radio, to play music while she worked.

She met Peter Watts, who was working on transhipping copper ore. Peter says he was UK born but came to Australia aged 6 as a "ten pound Pom" and is "South Australia bred". The ore came from Darwin to Larrimah by train, then was Trucked to Alice Springs. From there the train took the ore down to Marree where it was transferred to be transported on the standard gauge railway down to Adelaide for export.

Peter later worked painting railway cottages and would have a drink with Percy Dodd, Martha's father, who was always immaculately dressed. Percy would always have two longnecks. One night, he says, Peter said to Percy "I think I want to marry your daughter". Percy said "Talk to me tomorrow when you're sober". He did. Peter and Martha married in Adelaide in 1966.

Peter and Martha met at the old Marree Picture Theatre. Peter would be teased by Martha's baby sister who would call out "gecko coming" or "scarecrow coming" as he was often covered in residue and dust from his work. Both will be married 50 years on 28th June 2016.

Peter (junior) has a story about going out on the "tuk-a-tuk", the section car, with his young pals and some Arabana elders and his grand-dad Percy. They would go hunting up the train line, catch rabbits by throwing stones at them, and maybe cook them for lunch. They would then turn the tuk-a-tuk around and motor home.

On the very morning Grand-dad Percy died, Peter came out a bit late with his cousin and Percy had already gone. Percy had been head ganger out at Wangianna and Alberrie. Percy died on the job but the family say he would have lived had there been someone with acknowledge of first aid available.

Nowadays Peter and Martha live in suburban Adelaide. Peter is a very keen fisherman, not a pastime possible in Marree! Martha has the house as neat as a new pin - and no red sand to clear out.

Peter and Martha have three children, Peter (Junior), who is involved with Uncle Kevin Buzzacott in the anti-uranium movement, Dwyane who runs Boma's Graphics in Adelaide, and Amanda. Peter also works with Kurta Tirkandi - Learning Place within the TAFE system of South Australia which, inter alia, helps employers deal with the knowledge, beliefs and attitudes of their non-Aboriginal employees.

Dean Stuart

(interview in his home on 27th July 2014. Revised 14th April 2016 by telephone feedback).

Dean Stuart was born at Finniss Springs on 8th March 1945. He is a son of Laurie Stuart and Doreen Stuart, stepdaughter of Fred Strangways.

Fred had married Doris Baralda Strangways, mother of Doreen. Thus Dean counts his great grandmother as Laura Baralda and step grandfather as Fred Strangways, both Arabana.

Laurie was a son of Jack Hele and Louisa Ferguson, but Louisa later married Ted Stuart and the children took that name.

From Finniss Springs his family would go by horse and cart to visit Curdimurka, an important siding on the Ghan, where brother Len Stuart was working. They could see the Ghan coming for miles by the huge column of smoke. This was before the steam train was replaced by diesel in the mid 1950s. The children would be able to run across and buy chocolates and sweets from a window in one of the vans.

Dean was schooled at the UAM Mission school on Finniss Springs but left aged 14, with a Proficiency Certificate, the highest available qualification at the time. Dean then worked at the mission, doing jobs such as fencing. He and Grandfather Fred Strangways went then to Stuart's Creek on their horse and cart. then Coward Springs. Having asked head stockman Ernie Ellis they got pastoral jobs under Dick Nunn. He joined the Commonwealth Railways in 1963 aged 18, having put up his age, as one was not supposed to be recruited until age 21.

He worked with Uncle Syd Strangways at Wangianna, where Syd was the Ganger. They lived in fettler's cottages and monitored five miles of train line one way and five miles the other. Inspections were usually done twice a week. Any maintenance needing to be done was then assigned.

Sometimes there were emergencies such as a flood, washaway, sand over the line or a particular crisis, such as a derailment. Crow bars were used to prise the line back into alignment as required. (In the southern United States, these bars are called "Gandies" and the men are called "Gandy Dancers").

He worked back and forth from Wangianna to Stuart's Creek, alternating railway and pastoral work. He lived in the single men's quarters in Wangianna in 1963-4. Stores would be brought up from Port Augusta and he considers they "lived pretty high". He remembers the cook Barney "Combo" cooking stews, curries and making sweetdesserts. The gang would be given sandwiches for their lunch before setting off for the day on the tuk-a-tuk (motorised section car).

Dean Stuart (on the right) with Snooky Varcoe about 1963, standing in front of Syd Strangways car at Wangianna.
(Photograph courtesy of Dean Stuart)

He recalls a particular incline on the track leading to Wangianna near an underground water tank where the train would scrape the steel of the rails trying to get up. Uncle Syd used to sit atop the section car here and be pushed up the incline by two men on each side, just to get up Wangianna Hill. Dean can still recall Syd's famous words, as he sat perched on the old section car, in Arabana "yukapei" – let's go!

Later Dean worked from Marree down to Farina in the No 1 Gang on the standard gauge line.

Dean met Kitty (Katherine) in 1967 and they married in 1968. They have five children. Kitty's cousin Geoff Eames was a locomotive driver driving up to Alice Springs in the 1940s. She and her sisters-in-law, Pauline Thompson and Joy Dodd, were all train carriage cleaners at Marree.

Dean is now the Treasurer of the Arabana Aboriginal Corporation but has a major interest is reviving the Arabana language. He is working with Uncle Syd Strangways, following the lead from father Laurie and brother Rex Stuart who compiled a dictionary.

He has clear recollections of his grandmother mourning the loss of many babies who died in the epidemics that went through Arabana lands This may be the post World War I influenza pandemic or even the 1950s measles epidemic which killed a number of young people and babies. Mother Doreen sought to protect him by greasing him with emu fat.

He considers the railways were important in many ways for the Arabana. Obviously they linked the cattle industry with the wider world – cattle were shipped from Coward Springs. They did create a sort of dependence on the supply chain of goods from the Commonwealth Railway stores at Port Augusta, which can no longer occur. The railway allowed people of many nations to mix amicably.

Audrey Stewart (conversation on 18th June 2013 at Oodnadatta)

Audrey was born in June 1949 at Macumba Station, the daughter of Nellie Stewart (born 1932, Arrernte/Arabana people) and Pompey Reid, stockman on a cattle station (Antakarinja people). Uncle Sidney Stewart was a tribal man but worked on the railway in the 1960s. Because of pressure from the Department of Aboriginal Affairs, "the Welfare", the family moved to Oodnadatta in the late 1950s so the children could be sent to school. Meanwhile Audrey's dad worked at Allandale Station and did gardening in the town itself especially for Ben and Robyn Greenwood. Then Pompey became a police tracker and the family lived at the police station. (Bruce Shaw says that Audrey told him old Pompey went blind in 1966 aged 70). Their mother sewed them their clothes. Mother could speak Arrernte, Luritja, Arabana and English. Eventually she, sadly, became demented and died in a home in Port Augusta.

Oodnadatta itself is a meeting place for many tribes and corroborees continued until the 1960s. Eventually her own uncles banned the practices. Audrey says Oodnadatta is not Arabana land, although others dispute this.

She has been told that during WW2, Oodnadatta was a fueling stop for warplanes. The pilots and crew would give or throw blankets and food out of the plane as they passed over the Aboriginal camp. Her dad, Pompey, did not even know World War 2 was on!

Her paternal grandfather, her step-grandfather and father used to muster stock by horse, then they drove the sheep or cattle all the way from Alice to Marree. The Aboriginal stockmen, theoretically innumerate, could count up to three hundred sheep and also be aware if just one was missing. Stock would be taken across country from as far away as Birdsville. Once the railhead was reached, the stock would be taken to Adelaide.

Audrey herself worked as a cook for ringers so she could be near horses. She loved riding and was able to "tail the bullock", keep stock together in an unfenced area. By the 1950s cattle predominated and by 1990 motor bikes took over completely from horses.

Audrey is an Elder herself and her second oldest daughter is heir to the Dreamtime stories.

Audrey had a heart attack in 2008. Nowadays she is a Seventh Day Adventist and teaches about the evils of alcohol. She is growing healthy native plants in her own garden such as the Quandong. She would like her own biography to be heard, audiotaped and transcribed for future generations.

Professor Veronica Arbon, Director Wirltu Yarlu, University of Adelaide (conversations, over 2012 to 2014)

Veronica never worked on the train line herself but many family members did. Veronica was born on 23rd December 1950 at Alice Springs. Veronica travelled with her family from Port Augusta through Marree, where they changed from the silver Budd car to The Ghan.

Veronica Arbon (centre) 2013
(Photograph Courtesy of Melissa Nursey-Bray)

Genealogy: Veronica's Mother Shirley (now living in Darwin) married Ray Arbon and there were seven children, of whom Veronica is the eldest.

Veronica's maternal grandmother was Myra Hull (born 1914) who married maternal grandfather Charles "Geordie" Hodgson in 1930. Geordie was a white man from Tyneside, who worked as a ganger, then a porter and then a station master. Geordie was later a clerk on the railways at Marree. This "cross-racial" marriage was illegal at the time. Geordie and Myra had eleven surviving children. The eldest, Marjorie, married Phil Wallace and worked at the pub in Birdsville. Betty, the next, was sent to boarding school in Adelaide. Shirley helped to take care of the younger ones.

Veronica's maternal great grandmother was Clara (Mudlu) Strangways whose partner was William Hull (Yankunytjatjara is thought to be his heritage by some, although Veronica argues he is actually also Arabana).

William was the son of Adam Hull, a white store keeper from Mount Crawford, South Australia, and Ruby (Yankunytjatjara and Arabana as noted above) and was born about 1890, probably in Warrina where Adam Hull ran a small shop.

Clara's mother, so Veronica's great great grandmother was Lily Strangways (Arabana).

Extended Family: There are many maternal aunties and uncles: eight women and three men, including John Hodgson, the locomotive driver, about whom further information is of great interest to the family.

Veronica says that Uncle John was born in 1943 in Marree and worked on Urapunga Station as a young man with Ray Arbon, Shirley

Arbon's (nee Hodgson) husband. John was one of Aunt Shirley's younger brothers. He initially trained and worked as a stockman on Urapunga Station then worked on Elsey Station (*We of the Never Never*) before he went to Arabana country. Later he moved to live and work in the Northern Territory once again.

Uncle John trained in Port Augusta or Darwin as a locomotive driver but worked mainly in NT. He married Caroline Hayes in Adelaide. He mainly drove from Darwin to Larrimah and back.

Nanna Myra's sisters Daisy and Phyllis were placed in Nepabunna Mission. Their parents, William Hull and Clara, who sometimes worked at Coward Springs sought to get them out of the Mission with temporary success. There are letters to the Aboriginal Protector about this from these parents and from one of their older daughter Evelyn Hull's partner Sid Churches. However, the girls had to go back. They travelled on the train to return to the Misssion, permission being given in writing by the Police.

Nana Evelyn was the partner of Sid Churches, who ran the Coward Springs Hotel before it burnt down. According to Grandfather Geordie's son Douglas Hodgson (now deceased), Sid used to send a barrel of beer up to Alice Springs on the train for Geordie.

Railway information

Veronica says that there is a Seven Sisters Songline underlying the train route around Coward Springs and other places. Eileen Wingfield also says this is the case and is teaching a daughter about this highly significant Songline.

There were three railway houses near the current Telecentre in Marree. The Hodgson family lived in the nearest one next to where the current Telecentre now is when they moved from Oodnadatta to

Marree. This was when Grandfather Geordie was promoted to an Office job as Clerk.

Aboriginal people congregated near Warrina siding and Algebuckina, where there is permanent water, from what family have told Veronica. Algebuckina is a convergent point for a number of Dreamings. These include a Crane and Fish story from which her grandmother took her name. At Warrina there was a big camp on the north side of the Creek.

It is possible that the Arabana, when helping George Warren and John Ross survey for the train line, steered them away from some powerful sites, given that the route was altered from that which had been legislated.

Other information

Peake Station has a very powerful site not too far away, Veronica has been told.

Mount Hamilton Station near Wabma Kadarbu ("snake's head") mound springs had sixteen police sent in the early 1860s organised by the first John Warren. This was allegedly because Kuyani had bailed up whites and there was some fear expressed by those on Strangways Springs, as is recorded in the Warren letters (Arbon and Elders, 2010).

There is a song sung by Glen Hull in the book "Moonlight at Eva Creek" which relate to an Arabana train or car song and a lullaby. There is a still-known lullaby from a waterhole on the Macumba also recorded in this book. Lake Cadibarra Wirracanna (this is the shortened name; it means "stars dancing on water") north of the road between William Creek and Cooper Pedy, is also important to Arabana people due to the stories that belong to that place.

Veronica has been a member of the Ularaka, now Arabana Aboriginal Corporation. She became Director of Batchelor Institute in the Northern Territory and then Professor and Chair of Indigenous Knowledge Systems at Deakin University, Geelong. She is the sole author of "Arlathirnda, Ngurkarndha Ityirnda: being, knowing, doing: de-colonising indigenous tertiary education" (Arbon, 2008). She is co-author of "Wathili Family, Wilma Stories, Wadhlu Country", written with other Arabana Elders and published in 2010.

Having left Deakin, she became Professor and Director of Wirltu Yarlu at Adelaide University.

Wilfred Strangways

(conversation in Port Augusta, 27th of July, 2014)

Wilfred David Strangways was born in 1951, son of Bert Strangways and Ethel Wilton (Adnyamathantha).

Going back some three generations, Lily (Arabana) and Rang (Baguwida) had six children, including Henry (Wapili) Strangways. Wilfred's father Bert was a son of Henry (Wapili) Strangways and Edie Sargent (Arrernte).

I met with Wilfred in Port Augusta where he shared some of his recollections with me. Wilfred was born in Hawker but reared in Copley, where he went to school. Neither town is in Arabana country. His father Bert had an Exemption Certificate from 8th February 1950, and the family was consequentially "stuck in the middle", not allowed by law to associate with their Aboriginal kin, and not accepted by the white society either. In Copley they lived in a "tin shed".

The local school closed when he was in Year 7 and that was the end of schooling for him.

In 1966 the family moved to Port Augusta where Bert continued to work on the Railways, and was supplied with a house. Bert drove graders and other heavy plants.

Wilfred put up his age to join the Railways (a person was supposed to be aged 18) and spent five years as a shunter at Port Augusta. Later he trained at what he called "Bonehead College" in Port Augusta to become a guard. He then worked as an assistant guard, with a monthly run to Alice Springs on the Mixed (passenger and goods train).

In 1971 he was based at Port Augusta as an assistant guard when ninety Englishmen were recruited. They struggled with the heat, which was so hot you could fry an egg on the guard's van floor.

His son died and he hit rock bottom. He ended up in Adelaide. But he rallied and attended the Aboriginal Community College in 1978. He traced his relatives through Link-Up and has found relations all the way from Kadina, Adelaide, Alice Springs, Darwin and Marree.

Wilfred married Shirley Grantham and has two daughters by her. Corrinne is married to Henry Thompson and has two children. Cynthia, called Cindy, is married to David, called Jock, Anderson and has four daughters.

He remembers especially the glorious sight of Lake Eyre/Kati Thanda in flood in 1974 as he watched it from the train by a big full moon with its reflections in the water.

Wilfred Strangways::
(Photograph Courtesy of Melissa Nursey-Bray)

Nowadays Wilfred lives in Port Augusta in a house of his own, where he gets daily visits from daughter and grandchildren. He dreams of the railway days and recalls fondly memories of the mates he made.

Wilfred said that the railway track was laid directly on the bed of the Finke River, as a trial of putting in piles for a bridge had led them to just sink out of sight into the deep sands of the river bed. He gave me photographs of the track lying directly on the river sands.

Marilyn Ah Chee nee Hull, aka Hull-Stuart

(conversation on 24th June 2013 at Oodnadatta in the Pink Roadhouse)

Marilyn (dob 26/10/1953) is the daughter of Daisy Hull (Arabana, dob 22/7/1925 at Anna Creek) and Alec Kruger (born in 1924 at Katherine). Daisy had fifteen children and Marilyn was number 6.

Daisy was a daughter of Clara Strangways and William Hull. The other children of William and Clara were: Jessie Hull/Ah Chee, Myra Hull/Hodgson, Evelyn as noted, Glen Hull, Roy Hull, Daisy herself, Phyllis Marks, Gracie (b 7/6/33) Ah Fat/Warren and Millie Tanner. Daisy's children were June, Veronica, John, Jane, Irene, Marilyn then Kevin, Dorothy, Rowena, Ian, Sharon, Rosilyn, Debra, Lionel and Janette.

Daisy was Evelyn (Hull) Churches' younger sister. Evelyn had married Sid Churches at Curdimurka and they later ran the Coward Springs Hotel from 1937 to 1946. Other aunts include Betty Bowditch, Daphne May, Shirley, Lorraine Mills and Cathy, who all have memories of visiting there.

There was also Uncle Doug Hodgson, married to Shirley. Doug is a son of Geordie Hodgson and Myra nee Hull. (That is, he is Charlie Hodgson's uncle). Myra and Charles "Geordie" Hodgson, who died

2/7/66, had children Marjorie, Elizabeth, Shirley, Douglas, Pamela, John, Zena, Maureen, Daphne and Lorraine (see interview above with Betty and her sisters).

Clara herself was a daughter of Rang (Baguwida {died 1930}) Strangways {who had been examined by Dr Herbert Basedow in the 1920s at Anna Creek} and Lily (Arabana). William was a son of Adam Hull (white) and Ruby. Adam ran the shop at Warrina, a station on the Old Ghan. He lived in an old stone house and traded with Aboriginal people for dingo scalps, exchanging them for tea, sugar and so on. Ruby lived there for a while.

Rang and Lily's children were: Sarah (Gudjibuga) b 1880, d 1972; Henry (Wapili), b 1881, d 24/10/1961; Clara (Mudlu), b 1889, d 15/5/65; Tim (Midlangila), b 1891, d ?; Fred (Murili), b 1896, d 7/4/70; Sidney, b 1898, d?

Clara Hull was related to Rosie Ah Chee, nee Naylon. Clara died on 15th May 1965 at Port Augusta.

Marilyn's other grandmother was Sarah Hele nee Strangways, who married Andrew Hele (d 20/7/1958). Children were May, Dudley, Kathleen and Steve. Jennifer Newchurch counts herself as Arabana through father Steve. (Mother Audrey nee Eaglehawk was Pitjantjatjara). Steve Hele worked as a fettler.

Daisy and her younger sister Phyllis were of the Stolen Generations. Nanna had hidden the other children from the Welfare. Daisy was taken to Colebrook then Quorn and then went out to Mr and Mrs Eaton at Nepabunna (in Adnyamathanha country). She escaped aged 16. She went to Coward Springs where she helped Auntie Evelyn who had fallen sick.

Later Daisy went to Alice Springs and Marilyn was born there on 26th October 1953.

Later Evelyn split up with Sid Churches and married Henry Cox. They lived at Millers Creek Station. They reared one of Daisy's daughters, Deborah, and one Uncle's daughter, Charmaine.

Great Uncles Glen Hull and Roy Hull worked on the railways around Finniss Springs and Curdimurka.

Marilyn herself grew up with her mother and stepfather Mr Milera. He worked on the East West or transcontinental Railway at Pinba, Rawlinna and Deakin. Marilyn attended schools run by the railways. The railways were able to bring them clothes, food and entertainment. Welfare, who were the legal guardians of all Aboriginal Australians, never chased them. They were able to make their own toys and made their own fun. For instance, boxes were used as toy trucks.

Father Christmas used to come on the train each year with toys, a story later told in the delightful book *Tea and Sugar Christmas* by Jane Jolly, illustrated by Robert Ingpen (2014).

Many Aboriginal people did well from the railways. They were promoted, knowing the country, being able to survive the climate, being bush mechanics and could make do. Fettlers became gangers; gangers became train examiners and other critical positions.

Marilyn married Dean Ah Chee, who worked on the railway at Oodnadatta, later in Alice Springs. His father Charlie's family were railway people. They also worked at Perdika and Finke.

Oodnadatta was a boom town. It was a hub for many peoples but also a sad town as the Police and Welfare would bring Aboriginal children there and have them sent to Homes in Adelaide.

In the 1970s Marilyn worked on Carbine, the NSU diesel locomotive, in the train cleaning shed in Marree. She worked cleaning all the way from the guard's van to second and then first class carriages. There were about ten women doing this at the time, some with children. It was solid work when the train was in – but usually finished work cleaning by 2pm. There were about two trains a week then. There were also goods trains whereby she would clean the brake vans as well as carriages. Dining cars were made gleaming clean. Metal showers and toilets in sleeping cars had to be spotless.

If the supervisor was not satisfied the worker had to stay back and redo the whole carriage. There were two or three carriages per worker. The women would help each other out.

They were given their pay in cash in little envelopes, quite a lot of money for the time. They would place orders to buy goods made up in Port Augusta from the railway stores and sent up to them. Clothes, blankets and so on. All paid for with deductions from their pay.

Marilyn has two sons, Hayden and Phillip, neither of whom works on railways.

She is currently the Chair of Dunjiba, the Aboriginal organisation in Oodnadatta. They run the pub, the store, the museum, the dump and did run housing (which has been now moved to SA Housing). Health is under Health SA and the local clinic has one Registered Nurse and two Aboriginal Health Workers, one of whom speaks the local language. Aboriginal heritage is a key policy direction too. Marilyn is an enterprising and energetic person who is making a significant impact on Oodnadatta.

Lionel Dodd

(conversation on initial draft 26th July 2014, final correction 16th May 2016)

Lionel was born on 2nd March 1954, son of Percy "Nobby" Dodd (Arabana) and Sheila Strangways (Arabana). Percy himself was one of the sons of Amy (daughter of white pastoralist Francis Dunbar

Warren and Arabana lady Laura) and Tom Dodd, an Arrernte stockman.

His father Percy was a fettler in Marree.

One of Percy's responsibilities was to measure the faults along the line from Marree to Alice Springs on the "Chaser" train. He patrolled from Marree to Lyndhurst and up to Curdimurka, from time to time. His role involved fixing broken joints and other breakages.

Later Percy was relieving Ganger in Marree, No 2 Gang and was a relieving Ganger for Dave Warren (Arabana) when Dave was out on Patrol.

Percy died on the job.

Sheila, Lionel's mother, was the daughter of Henry Wapili Strangways (Arabana) and Edie Sargent (Southern Arrernte).

As a youngster Lionel broke his leg and was hospitalised at the Children's Hospital in Adelaide. "His parents were able to come and stay nearby. He was transferred for convalescence to Escort House", said Lionel's sister Martha.

In his childhood school years, Lionel lived in a cottage on the western side beside the train line at the south end of Marree. Marree was by then a change of gauge station, from standard to narrow gauge.

Lionel would spend his school holidays at Finniss Springs or at Stuart Creek with his Uncle Norm and Auntie Jean.

He was recruited into the Commonwealth Railways in the 1970s after a number of other jobs.

Lionel tended to move back and forth from pastoral to railway work. He started in the Yard Gang in Marree, then worked as fettler at Curdimurka, Beresford and Alberrie Creek. Then, after gaining his Ganger Certificate, on 23rd November 1977, worked as a Ganger at William Creek.

Lionel at the Copber Pedy race Meeting 1980
(Photograph Courtesy of Lionel Dodd)

He recalls the big floods in 1974. He was living in Stuart's Creek at the time, working as a stockman.

While staying with Uncle Syd Strangways in Alice Springs, he did start training as a locomotive driver but left before completing the course. Also while staying up in Alice Springs he played for South Alice Football Club.

Lionel recalls one big derailment north of Finniss which delayed trains for a week, or perhaps 3-4 days. He was sent down from Alice Springs on a workers' train with his Uncle Syd Strangways and Kevin Buzzacott to help with the derailment and fixing the line.

Whilst working at William Creek he met his New Zealand born wife Susan Hill. He married Susan in 1979 and they eventually had seven children of their own.

The old Ghan closed in 1983 and the lines from Alice Springs to Leigh Creek were torn up over the next three years.

After leaving William Creek at the close of the Ghan line from Port Augusta to Alice Springs, he worked on Anna Creek Station, later for the Highways Department and on a dairy farm in New Zealand for about ten years.

The Premier of the day, Sir Thomas Playford with Mr Percy Dodd at the opening of the new standard gauge line, in Marree in 1957.
Lionel, his youngest son (centre).

In more recent years he has been a bus driver for Light City Buses which is part of Transfield.

Paul Tanner

(conversation on 16th October 2014 at Finniss Springs)

Paul is the current Chairman of the Arabana Aboriginal Corporation. He was on the railways for sixteen years from 1975. He was born 1st September 1955, eldest son of Mildred, nee Hull and Frederick Tanner.

Paul went to Darwin after Cyclone Tracy in 1975 with his cousin brother (their mothers Mildred and Myra were sisters), John Hodgson. A year on in 1975 after Cyclone Tracy, Darwin was still a bit of a mess so he worked with various contractors tidying up and then joined the Australian National Railways in the goods sheds. John O'Donohue was the manager at the time. He met and worked with some Torres Strait Islanders. Unfortunately he hasn't seen them since but they were great blokes. There he worked loading and unloading goods with Trans-Shipping. He worked on the gantry crane unloading road trains for about a year but when the train line to Katherine closed he transferred back to Port Augusta.

Back in Port Augusta he started at the bottom sweeping the platform and number-nicking, but undertook schooling upstairs in the Railway Station and was eventually promoted to shunter. He spent a lot of time at Marree relieving as shunter, yardmaster and also as an assistant guard on the old North line to Alice Springs. When travelling by rail in summer, he was in a non-airconditioned brake van which had the thermometer nearly bursting out of the top. You could cook an egg on flat-tops as it was so hot. He worked along the line on the slow- mixed (passengers and goods) to Alice Springs and would be away from one to three weeks. Washaways would obviously delay his return to family.

He also relieved as Station Assistant at Finke and Oodnadatta. He spent some time on the East-West line.

Paul Tanner with Sydney Strangways at the re-naming of Kati Thanda - Lake Eyre, Standing along the edge of the lake where the Oondattada Track and the old ghan line run parallel.

(Photograph Courtesy of Susan SP Dodd)

Later Paul became a leading shunter based back in Port Augusta as he was tired of being away from family and living out of a tucker-box and suitcase. It was still shift work, and sometimes the Yardmaster would get them up at 4am because that is when the train had got in.

The life with Australian National Railways was hindered by inefficiency. Sometimes a gang would be left without a Section Car on the old north line, and just while away the time until one was provided.

All his uncles worked on the railways, in those days men could walk in off the street and get a job fettling or shunting. Sadly concrete sleepers reduced the need for fettlers and employment opportunities decreased and morale did decline. It was a bit like motor bikes and helicopters reducing the need for a man on a horse as a stockman.

Off duty time was spent with family as much as possible, mainly in Marree.

Paul was present on the platform in Marree when the last Ghan train came through in 1983. The place was "packed". After this lined closed completely many Arabana went to work on the other lines - the East-West now Indian-Pacific, the relocated Ghan running through Tarcoola and the line in the Northern Territory, which finally was joined north to south after he had left.

He worked on the railways for sixteen years from 1975.

Upon leaving the railways in 1991 Paul moved to work in the Justice system. He has worked extensively with Indigenous Courts for both Nungas and other Aboriginal peoples throughout SA..

Paul is married with two daughters, Kathryn and Rebecca, neither of whom have worked in the rail system.

Charlie Hodgson (conversation about the Old Ghan Line, Alice Springs, 11th March 2012).

Men's Health Coordinator, Central Australia Remote Health Services, Department of Health

Charlie said he is aged 47 years (dob 1/8/1966). The old Ghan stopped in 1981 and he had no personal recollection of this train line but a lot of other information, especially about the times before the train.

Explorer John McDouall Stuart had a young male Arabana guide (name unknown) for his First Expedition (14th May 1858 to 11th September1858). {This information, although without the designation of the young man as being Arabana, is also given on the John McDouall Stuart Society website [http://johnmcdouallstuart.org.au/ first-five- expeditions] }.

Charlie said that this young man was killed by Arabana elders between the First and Second Expeditions (this latter from April to July 1859) because he had revealed secret information such as the whereabouts of sacred waterholes and mound springs. The Second Expedition revealed what Stuart thought of as virgin land, "wonderful country,... scarcely to be believed" which he claimed as a pastoral lease. Charlie asserted that Arabana people were killed on this Second Expedition. (It is possible that this time in 1859 is when a Smallpox Epidemic swept through the Arabana for the first time {Dick Kimber}. It is said by the John McDouall Stuart Society that there was conflict with the Warramunga {near Tennant Creek} further north on the Third Expedition on 26th June 1860).

Pastoral stations followed virtually immediately after the explorers. The first, Strangways, was established in 1863. Arabana people later moved into the towns along the old Ghan because their water supplies had been taken over by the pastoralists. They worked on the railway from 1884 as one of the very few alternatives, to feed their families. Strangways, Anna Creek and Finniss Springs Stations were, however, supportive of Arabana people. Aboriginal people elsewhere had been shot, which fact was known to Arabana.

From 1866 Afghans and their camels traversed Arabana land taking supplies to pastoral stations. The Arabana did not mingle with these non-Aboriginal people for some time but then did marry Afghans and there are a number of genealogies with Afghan names who are now claimed as Arabana people (endorsed by Pamela Rajkowski in her books). Dieri women also married Afghans.

Old Trading Routes, Dreaming Routes or Songlines were traversed by Afghans, especially the *Chilpa* or Quoll line. The Overland Telegraph Line (built between 1870 and 1872) followed by the Railway (through Arabana country from 1884 onwards) followed these lines as well, because there was water along that way and few others along the west of Lake Eyre.

John Hodgson who later became the first Arabana locomotive driver
(Photograph Courtesy of Professor Veronica Arbon)

Charlie's paternal grandfather Charles "Geordie" Hodgson (from Northumberland), was a clerk on the Railways. Paternal grandmother was Myra Hull, the daughter of Clara Hull, the daughter of Lily Strangways, who was Arabana.

Charles and Myra had eight daughters and three sons, including Charlie's father John, who later became the first Arabana locomotive driver (probably late 1960s or early 1970s). John Hodgson worked mainly on the Northern Railway around Darwin. John and his wife had several children, including Charlie.

Charlie's mother was the great-granddaughter of George Hayes, a linesman for the OTL, and a Kaytetye lady from near Barrow Creek Barrow Creek was a telegraph station from 1872. Maternal grandmother came from Neutral Junction Station.

The pastoral stations along the old Ghan line "fed the armies of the world" during World War 2 with sheep and cattle both transported to Adelaide and for the huge numbers of service personnel, including many Black Americans, who came through the Centre during the War.

Charlie's father John Hodgson was a shunter at Marree (along with Kenny Dodd). He did an engineering course from about 1968 to 1970 to become a locomotive driver. Charlie is very keen to find confirmatory information about this so that he can have one of the new Ghan locomotives named after his father. Charlie does have some pay books which would be useful to check dates etc. I was able to confirm this information by a visit to the National Australian Archive at Chester Hill in Sydney (see Appendix 4).

Dennis Amos

(conversation at Finniss Springs on 18th October 2014).

Dennis was born on 16th September 1961, later in his father's life, he being aged fifty at the time. His father reminisced about being born at Warrina in Arabana country and when fettlers were still called by the English title of "navvies" (short for navigational engineers and from a time when this group of workers built canals). Dennis was reared in Port Augusta, where many Arabana have lived and still do. He and family would go to Finniss Springs for holidays. Sometimes this would be with brother-in-law Clarrie Warren.

Joining the Commonwealth Railways in 1979 in Western Australia, Dennis worked replacing wooden sleepers with concrete ones for the East-West line between Kalgoorlie and Port Augusta. He was in a special gang of up to sixty men. The old sleepers would have to be taken out by hand with pick and shovel, although there was machinery to help insert the new concrete sleepers. He worked on this job for about a year.

Dennis then worked welding the rails to eliminate the "clicketty-click". He worked at Hughes doing this. He then moved back to Port Augusta where he worked upon buildings for a year or so. It was there he met partner Glenys. They have three children: Mark, Jacinda and James.

He rejoined the railways working as a fettler at Barton on the East-West line in 1985. They lived in a railway house where the rent was a modest $20 per fortnight. They had to supply their own furniture but there was free electricity - but no air conditioning. He worked his way up to become Road Foreman with a team of twelve under him. They'd do big jobs such as derailments.

Dennis Amos 2015
(Photograph Courtesy of Susan SP Dodd)

In 1987 they moved to Tarcoola so that son Mark could attend school. They were there for nine years then left and moved away from rail work. Dennis then worked on Highways based in Port Augusta. He worked on the Birdsville and Strzelecki Tracks, as well as the William Creek to Coober Pedy Road.

He moved back to rail work on the Leigh Creek line from 1998 until 2005, using his skills as a welder. This railway is on the same route as part of the old Ghan line. Dennis then came to Victoria where he worked on the railway at Sale, doing re-railing between Sale and Bairnsdale. He would be away for a fortnight then return home.

He was then again on the Highways as a plant operator preparing roads at the Prominent Hill and Iluka mines.

Dennis retired on the grounds of ill health in 2009.

Both sons Mark and James did work upon the railways for a while, but are now truckdrivers.

Aaron Stuart (conversation on 28th July 2014 in Port Augusta)
Director of the Arabana Aboriginal Corporation and principal for the second Arabana Native Title Claim.

"I was born in 1968. My father was Rex Stuart (born on Finniss Springs, died 2001), a fettler on the Old Ghan both in Marree and Port Augusta, and my mother was Angeline Shirley Mackenzie, Adnyamathanha, from the Flinders ranges, Wirrealpa Station. I was third of five children: eldest was Dawn, then Noblelene, then me, then Virginia and finally Corrinna.

"My paternal grandfather was Laurie Stuart (died 2006) who was himself the son of Jack Hele and Louisa Ferguson. Louisa later married Tom Stuart and the children took his name. Paternal grandmother Doreen was a daughter of Doris, daughter of Fred Strangways and Laura Baralda. My maternal grandmother was Ruth, from Eringa, Bloods Creek.

"Louisa moved from Peake to Mount Dutton probably because of an epidemic affecting the Aboriginal families. (*This may be the 1950s measles epidemic*). There is a siding towards Oodnadatta, and about 4-5 Km away is a little valley with 8-9 humpies, still visible. The families who survived later moved to Oodnadatta.

"Finniss Springs had two sides: there was Francis Dunbar Warren's Aboriginal family, with houses, being given rations, and attending school and church. On the other side of the creek there were more transient Aboriginal families.

"Lots of my uncles and aunties worked on and were paid by the railways. Robert Anthony Stuart (dob 17/7/1952), Lenard Stuart (dob 2/3/1957) and Locky Stuart (1/1/1948). Also twin Stewarts, Henry (dob 12/3/1926) and Sydney (dob 12/3/1926) all of whom would have personnel records.

Rex Stuart with his three children, Corrina, Virginia and Aaron, at Marree (Photograph Courtesy of Aaron Stuart and family ©)

"I was put into a "home" for five years as a child at Umeewarra, on the Davenport Reserve.

"Marree was then a change of gauge station. Passengers on the Old Ghan used to get out of the silver carriages which had come up from Adelaide and transfer to the old wooden ones with leather seats, squeaky, dark inside, like in old British movies.

"One memory I have when I was aged 8 or 9 was going out with my dad, grandfather, a strong man, and my uncle looking for gold at Edward's Creek near Warrina Siding. It was midsummer and about 47 degrees. Grandfather used to get gold and sell it to the rail workers so he could buy food. We had a gold detector machine. My grandfather didn't usually swear but he looked at this contraption and said 'that turnout may be shit, eh!'.

"Another memory is of getting into mischief. Us kids used to take a section car and go for rides up the line – hoping no train would come. One day we got caught by the fettlers because we didn't put it back in time. Got a bit of a flogging over that one.

"Older blokes used to pinch petrol from the railways to go hunting. It had a dye in it so it looked a different colour from normal petrol. Never seemed to get caught.

"The train brought us new clothes, new people and was exciting for a boy living in a small country town. The train provided fun. The smell of diesel, the sound of the old NSU train idling sounding like a watch, then powering up are all imprinted on my memory. There were several different types of train: the Old Ghan, also known as the Flash Ghan, passengers only with perhaps some cars, the mixed which had freight and some passengers and the pure goods and stock trains.

"The final Old Ghan from Alice Springs to Marree ran in 1983, the centenary of the line starting. I saw the line being torn up when I was perhaps 12, 14 years old. Ray Gosse, an original contractor to do this, still lives in Marree. Freight trains and stock trains continued for another three years up to Marree before the rest of the line was torn up. The train stopping was a big blow to the town of Marree. The population went down, the school had fewer children. You can see a photo of me as a schoolboy in Lois Litchfield's book (*possibly page 26 back row on the left*). Later there were race meetings and special events but it was not the same.

"There is a photograph of me at the first train to run all the way to Darwin, both with my big hat on and the memorial baseball cap (which Aaron showed me). By then Aboriginal people needed to be acknowledged".

Aaron Stuart at opening of New Ghan 2004
(Photograph Courtesy of Aaron Stuart)

Peter Watts

(conversation on 25/5/2013 at Lake Eyre/Kati Thanda).

Peter is the son of Peter Watts (senior), non-Indigenous, who worked on the railway, and Martha nee Dodd, former train cleaner, Arabana (see above). His maternal Grandfather was Percy Dodd, also a rail worker, being a head ganger working out of Wangianna and Alberrie Creek. Other siblings were Dwyane and Amanda.

Peter recalls going on holidays to Finniss Springs and Anna Creek. They would go out on Section Cars and go hunting directly off the railway track. They could fling stones and hit the numerous rabbits. Fox hunting was also undertaken, and quite lucrative.

In either 1977 or 1978 he and a cousin walked out to the shed to find a Section car missing. Old Grandfather Percy had gone to Alberrie and died there.

Peter had family on many sidings: Wangianna, Alberrie, Coward Springs, Curdimurka, Beresford, Strangways and William Creek. The furthest set of relatives were at Macumba.

The railways were fun for him as a young boy.

Jodie Warren (conversation on 14th June 2013 in Marree).

Jodie, born in 1969, is the daughter of Stan Warren, youngest brother of Arthur Warren and his second wife Dora Stuart. Jodie now lives in Marree and is involved with the Arabana Aboriginal Corporation.

Her recollection of Francis Dunbar Warren's other children by Laura Baralda (died about 1945) are Mona or Merna (Merrick) b 1912, Angus Warren b 1915, Amy (Dodd, Reg Dodd's mother), Dave Warren b 1921, Fiona (Murray) and then Stan Warren, her own father, b 1925.

Father Stan had been a drover. The family lived on Finniss Springs Station from her birth to about 1978, having been running the Station after Francis Dunbar Warren died in 1958. Joanne's siblings are Darren, Leonie, Gregory, Justin and Clinton and half-sibs are Dorothy, Isabel, Wayne, Roger, Christopher and Francis.

Norman Woods and Stan Warren
(Photograph Courtesy of Aaron Stuart)

Jodie (also known as Joanne) recalls her childhood as a railway child from about 1978. They used to live near the tennis courts near the platform of the railway station in Marree. She recalls exciting evenings when the Ghan arrived bringing visitors who alighted for an hour while changing to the narrow gauge railway which proceeded to Alice Springs from Marree. Travellers liked to take photographs of the Aboriginal children. There was also the "mixed" train which brought rations and other goods for the rail workers themselves.

Also living there in Marree at the time was Dave Warren, ganger, with his family. Dave's son Terrence was particularly mentioned. Also in Marree was Reg Dodd, by that time train examiner. The gangers at Alberrie were very generous to Stan's family. Stan had friends and relations all the way up the line.

The family moved to Stirling North then Port Augusta where Stan worked as a train cleaner for many years until he retired in the 1990s. Jodie and her two elder sisters were on the centenary Ghan train from Stirling North all the way to Marree in 1983.

Jodie is of the view that life was less hard for Arabana rail workers and their families than it had been for other Arabana or other Aboriginal Australians.

Kyle Dadleh

(conversation in University Lodge, Carlton, Melbourne on 9th December 2011)

Kyle is a grandson of Reg Dodd (Arabana Elder), being a son of Jackie, Reg's daughter and Alan Dadleh, boilermaker/welder. He has a brother Courtley, who works at Leigh Creek Coal Mine, who has been the apprentice of his own father as a boilermaker/metal fabricator. His paternal grandparents are Ronnie Dadleh (who identifies as Afghan) and Sue.

He is graduate of Trinity Grammar, Melbourne, which city is now his home. He had obtained a scholarship from Trinity College to undertake his tertiary education.

Kyle was brought up at Leigh Creek but spent most holidays at Marree. He also spent time at Alberrie Creek siding and recalls the Ghan coming through, with all the children waving from trackside.

He has been told of the first diesel which came through in 1954. Leigh Creek itself, the township, was moved six kilometres south when the mine expanded.

Kyle recalls fossicking beside and near the old train line. The track bed was raised and is still visible most of the way along the old Ghan line. There were water tanks at regular intervals, some still in evidence. There is evidence of old beaches and sea and lake floor. Fossilised ripples are tilted, showing ancient earth movements.

He used to find old coins, medicine bottles and other types of bottle. There were ancient fireplaces and fossil worms in petrified wood. There were many artefacts and bones to be found.

Marree, he recalls, was split into two sections, the "white" and "Afghan/Aboriginal" sides.

Kyle had a bit part in a movie, "Serenades", released in 2001, playing an "Afghan boy". This film was made in the same area as "Rabbit-Proof Fence".

Nowadays he works in commercial leasing and property management and sales. He was a political candidate in 2010 for the Liberal Party.

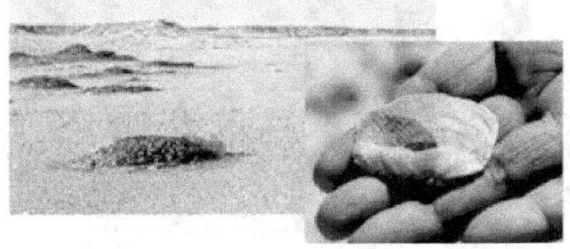

Evidence of old beaches.
(Photographs courtesy of Susan SP Dodd)

Aboriginal men and women at a train stop. The men have decorative head dress and are holding weapons: taken sometime between 1916-1932.

(Photograph courtesy of the State Library of South Australia. SLSA: B 53762)

Two steam locomotives which collided near Stranways Springs, February 1943.

(Photograph courtesy of the State Library of South Australia. SLSA: B 57501)

William Creek Railway Station: taken sometime between 1916-1932
(Photograph courtesy of the State Library of South Australia. SLSA: PRG 1559/8/8)

6

ARABANA MAKING HISTORY

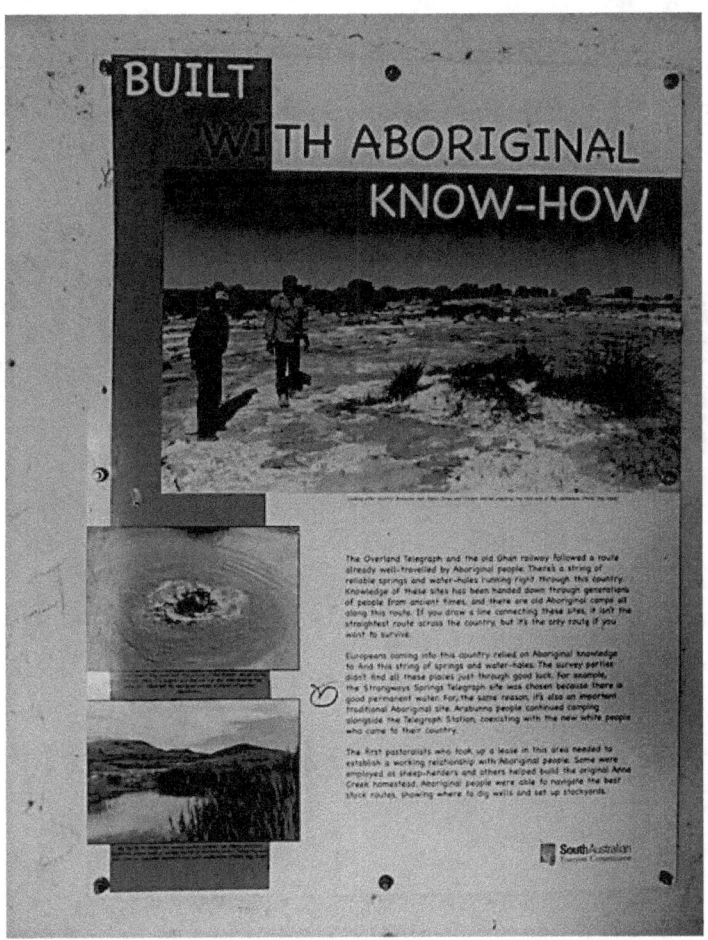

Photograph of sign along the Oodnadatta Track (2013).

Aaron Stuart is a Director of the Arabana Aboriginal Corporation. He was present as an honoured guest on 1st February 2004 when the New Ghan made its first trip from Adelaide to Darwin. The hundred year project had finally come to pass. By this time, Aboriginal people were on the scene, front and centre. In 1957 Arabana had been on hand as seemingly marginal spectators when the Standard Gauge rail track made it to Marree, but at that stage their significant contribution as workers was not acknowledged. The change in that half century was part of larger political shifts but left unknown the true story of Arabana on the Ghan.

A team of men lifting a large section of railway track during a repair operation
(Photograph courtesy of the State Library of South Australia. SLSA: PRG 280)

Railway houses, Marree Approximately 1924
(Photograph courtesy of the State Library of South Australia. SLSA: B 50361)

How did Arabana survive and thrive after several devastating blows to their people and culture starting from the 1850s? Most pastoralists around the west of Kati Thanda/Lake Eyre did not offer Arabana any more than subordinate existence. There were cordial relations and mutual adaptations between the settlers and Arabana, but landholder Frances Dunbar Warren, in the early twentieth century, was an exception to this general rule. He was a strong proponent for the local Aboriginal Australians and had his Aboriginal family and many unrelated other Aboriginal Australians with him on the re-established Finniss Springs Station.

The coming of the railway, however, routinely offered more and better prospects than pastoralism. These opportunities were seized by the Arabana. Even the original survey for the Ghan line included Arabana. There was equal participation as a worker, in the western sense of wages and conditions, from the 1920s. Rail offered education beyond the skills to be pastoral landholders' employees, near serfdom. The railway provided a pathway for a future beyond the passing of the train line itself. Arabana have subsequently moved into skilled trades, academia, into tertiary educated professions and other aspects of the Australian economy without shedding their self-asserted Aboriginal identity.

There has been a settler-colonialist backlash to equal participation with restrictions and racism continuing into the present day, but Arabana have organised to meet this. How have they done this?

Cultural historian Edward S Casey, writing in 1993, averred "Every culture has its place in some natural region, however much that region has been devastated and levelled into a scene of sites. Culture, that last fastness of the collective ego, reconnects, despite itself, with a wild realm of natural places. In order to sustain and renew itself, it must touch base with the wild earth from which it arises."

Arabana would, however, contest that their realm was "wild" in any ordinary sense of the word (untamed, unoccupied), because it was and remains a storied landscape, with well-known places of former agriculture, Ancestral Beings' activities (who include animal and totemic beings) and journeys, and actual placement in the landscape. Nonetheless the insistence that Casey has of the primacy of place is an important notion for all peoples. The railway ran from Marree to Oodnadatta as a literal iron rod through the heart of Arabana country. Every aspect of life was affected by the train line. But contrariwise also the train line itself was affected by the Arabana. They were never just ghosts or spectators. Their sacred sites and mound springs, shown to Europeans, determined the route of the Old Ghan. They fed the construction crews. They worked on the Old Ghan line from the start, including its infrastructure, its engines and rolling stock until the line was discontinued, a period of 100 years. They travelled to transact customary and contemporary business on the train itself. They transcended the construct of being "on the sidelines" and participated in the dominant economy on their own terms. Arabana took a different road, the collective iron road.

This is a more nuanced history than a monolithic thrust to civil and then land rights. Arabana were participants into the world of the settler colonists straight away from 1884 onwards, rather than being a subordinate part of the pastoral landscape and neo-Europeanisation of their country. Professor Lynn Russell has argued in her 2012 book, *Roving Mariners*, that the coast and the seas are "liminal spaces" where interactions between colonisers and colonised are more flexible than other domains. People are recognised for their skills, not just as a group to be used and controlled. Individuals have a degree of agency even within a more generally oppressive society. The corridor of the railway offered a similar opportunity.

Latterly the Arabana have gained Native Title to most of their old traditional lands, which has been important to the older people in particular. They have gained leasehold over the old Finniss Springs Station and Mission. The titles are not freehold, nor Torrens Title, and are held by an organisation, the Arabana Aboriginal Corporation, not individuals. This is not necessarily an unalloyed step forward. It can in some ways hinder things. For instance, Australian law now makes public thoroughfares exempt from Native Title claims. The very Dreaming Tracks which led settlers into Arabana lands remain stolen. These corridors are literally different spaces. Arabana use them "like everybody else", but cannot, under this "law", belong to or own them. Torrens Title, devised by Sir Robert Torrens in 1858, captures ALL interests in a property, including transfers, mortgages, leases, elements, covenants, resumptions and other rights in a single Certificate of Title. It constitutes, once registered with the State, indefeasible evidence of title. Metaphorically, it is as if the Arabana now own the body but not the arteries of their own land.

Moreover, the Arabana under Native Title cannot develop their land but only practice traditional activities such as hunting, fishing and gathering. For instance, a commercial Solar Farm on most of Arabana land could fuel all of South Australia, but is not legally possible except perhaps on the leased Finniss Springs itself. The Act limits Arabana on traditional lands to traditional activities leading to subsistence. There has been agreement by the Corporation to mining exploration well away from Finniss Springs, which had also been carried out on that station in the 1920s or so, but no commercial venture has yet eventuated. Fortunately Arabana people have diversified, moving to many places and professions: miners at Leigh Creek and Roxby Downs, bus drivers in Adelaide and elsewhere, conservation officers, truck drivers, real estate manager in Melbourne, tour guide, justice officer in Port Augusta, hospitality staff, dancer, actor, playwright, fashionista, academic professor, and so on.

Another value held by the white people is reading and writing (literacy) which gives access to knowledge other than the more secret orally transmitted knowledge that Arabana traditionally used. When Francis Dunbar Warren allowed a Mission on Finniss Springs in 1939, and when the United Aborigines Mission established their children's home establishment in Oodnadatta in 1924, the resulting literacy and numeracy expanded opportunities on the railway and elsewhere. Knowledge of this "whitefella" skill set is power in a very literal sense on the railway - an Arabana locomotive engineer will actually control the levers that run this massive powerful engine. Adding to traditional modes of knowledge such as tracking and information about plants and animals, the sky and the seasons, plus the metaphysical world of ancestors and Dreamtime stories, literacy multiplied Arabana options.

And a train travels much faster than any earlier modes of transport. As noted, a journey from Alice Springs to Adelaide, which formerly took six weeks, could be undertaken in three days. This increase in mobility is another emblem of western-ness that Arabana embraced from the time the railway arrived. Ochre pilgrimages were done in rapid safe comfort; visiting relatives up and down the line became normative. It increased contact with other Aboriginal peoples. Moreover, speed and steam are synonymous for the Victorian mind with the concept "progress", highly valued! Working and travelling on the train, metonym for progress itself, meant Arabana were, to a degree, on the same social level as white people. It is highly ironic that the train became called "the Ghan", as cameleers just walk everywhere with their beasts of burden. This pace is the one which humans have used since they became this species. Cameleers are not symbols of "progress" as the train is with its elements of speed, its greediness for water and huge carrying capacity. Train riding and working Arabana leap into modernity.

Again, in the late 1920s, when the extension of the railway from Oodnadatta to Alice Springs was being built, and the railway to Perth had been running since 1917, the South Australian Parliament passed a regulation forbidding Aborigines from proximity to the railway unless they had legitimate business there. Not only did this seek to push back the tide of "modernity" from involving Aboriginal peoples, and fly in the face of the reality in Northern South Australia, but probably marks the nadir of alienation and racism in that State. But by then Arabana were already participants.

In the present day Arabana, descendants of the enterprising survivors of the transport and cultural revolutions, have internalised the iron rod to be their own backbone: strong, flexible, bearing heavy loads, with vision beyond the narrow compass of the line itself. This book has shown the paradoxical effect that the train was indeed good for the Arabana. The book provides a counterweight instance to the many stories of continued remorseless negative aftermath of Australian colonisation and colonialism. The Arabana now have signs up along the train route celebrating that the Ghan was constructed and maintained with "Aboriginal knowhow". The Arabana, like many Indigenous Australians, were major contributors in this nation's development.

Section of abandoned track, Arabana country
(Photograph courtesy of Susan SP Dodd)

APPENDIX 1

RAILWAYS AND OTHER INDIGENOUS PEOPLES IN AUSTRALIA:

The Age Of Steam Enters The Dreaming

It is impossible for anyone to ignore the presence and contribution of railways to Australia's development. This Appendix considers the contribution of other Indigenous peoples in this development throughout the states and territories of Australia, particularly in the parts of South Australia beyond Arabana country. The railways were important in the spread of white settlement throughout Australia The period from 1863 to 1912 witnessed the building of most of Australia's major railway lines. There was a further burst of construction activity after World War II when mining companies around Australia built and used railways to transport their ores to port facilities. An even later development, connected to the thesis, was the construction of the "new Ghan" line, connecting Alice Springs to Darwin, which was completed in 2004. As this chapter suggests, the Indigenous peoples contributed both to the construction and servicing of these railways. Indeed, in the period between 1863 and 1912 the age of steam entered the Dreamtime; and in the case of the Ghan followed the Indigenous peoples' trade routes and Songlines. However, unlike in the pastoral industry, the contributions of Indigenous peoples in these developments have not been fully recognized in Australia's history. This chapter seeks to redress this by exploring the stories of Indigenous people who were involved in building, servicing and maintaining railways throughout the States and Territories.

New South Wales (settled by white people 1788)

The official history of *The Railways of New South Wales 1855-1955* (Paddison, 1955) does not mention Aboriginal people at all. Paddison's history of the state's railways is dated and was published at a time when Indigenous Australians had no place in the nation's White Australia histories. However, a 2011 brochure published by the Barani Barabugu organisation asserts that Indigenous people played a greater part in the expansion of the railways in New South Wales than given credit for in the official account (Barani Barabugu Walk Brochure June 2011). Given the absence of Indigenous labour in the official history, these pieces of ephemera are important in beginning to gain an insight into their contribution in the development of rail in New South Wales.

The construction of the railways in Sydney and its surrounding areas started in 1855. At this time, a number of Aboriginal people were said to be living near Cleveland Paddock in Redfern, which became the location for railyards and Eveleigh Workshops. Building of the workshops commenced in 1882 and they were finally opened in 1886. Eveleigh railway yards was Sydney's largest employer from the time it opened and one of the biggest employers of Aboriginal people living in Sydney. Many Aboriginal men also worked in the Alexandria goods yard loading trains with kegs and potatoes and on the waterfront docks at Walsh Bay and Darling Harbour (Barani Barabugu brochure). Following the closure of the Eveleigh railway yards in the 1980s, the former workshops on either side of the railway line were converted for other uses. On the southern side in the former locomotive Workshops is the Australian Technology Park, and on the northern side is Carriage Works, a hub for contemporary arts and culture. At both sites, there is information exhibited that describes some of the work practices that took place here. Indigenous people can be seen in photographs there but their contributions have yet to be fully explored.

Michael Davis has written "Aboriginal Connections with Eveleigh: a report prepared for the Sydney Metropolitan Development Authority" in 2012. Regrettably, as he says, "details of Aboriginal workers at the Workshops have yet to be established, (*but*) it is known that the site was an important focus for employment for Aboriginal people". Professor Lucy Taksa alludes to Aboriginal workers in her academic papers but again has negligible documentary confirmation for the Eveleigh Workshops. Possibly local Gadigal people worked there, although most workers would certainly have been incomers from rural NSW, displaced by pastoralists, and their descendants. Davis also states that hundreds of Aboriginal people travelled from their own lands to work in the boiler room, foundry and goods yards. Given the discrimination against Aboriginal peoples, and regime of forced removals from family after the crossing of the Blue Mountains in 1812, many would have been reluctant to reveal their Indigeneity. Hence the Indigenous contribution has been 'whited-out' of the history.

However, there are individual memoirs that tell the stories of Indigenous rail workers. These men, as the records show although women certainly worked on railways too, worked outside their own country, and thus differ in their experiences from Arabana who mostly were able to stay where they were from.

Vince Wenberg, probably Yaegl people, born in 1932 at Ulgundahi Island, Maclean, New South Wales, (Oral History Project 2001; stolengenerationstestimonies.com/testimonies/1000.html) was removed from his family aged 8 and placed at La Perouse, Sydney. With a foster family briefly, he was reunited with family before again being removed and sent to Kinchela in Kempsey in 1944. He joined the railways in 1954 (Oral History Project, 2001, p20). He started in the Eveleigh Workshops, then joined the millwrights' section then became a brickies' labourer. In 1956 he joined the Eveleigh Running Sheds, starting as a cleaner. He passed the exam for fireman and was promoted to locomotive driver in 1960. He drove both freight and passenger trains all over the State. He stayed with the railways until retiring in 1993. Wenberg retired from the New South Wales railways in 1993. His story surfaced as one of the Stolen Generations' testimonies as noted above. The experience of forced removals from his family had instilled in Wenberg a reticence about revealing his Indigeneity. His story offers insights into why the indigenous contribution to the railway is missing from the history. The past has taught the like of Wenberg to hide their Indigeneity if they wished to advance in white Australian society. In more recent times a daughter of his also became an engine driver.

Bandjalung elder Charles Harold Moran, born 1930, in his autobiography (2004, pp 91-2, 109-12, 114 and 129-31) says that the

> NSW and Queensland railways employed many Aboriginal people, including his brother Peter and himself. Moran recalled these people working in a variety of capacities, including engine drivers, stokers (firemen), waitresses, guards and track foremen (ganger) and fettlers. His own work duration in the railway system was, however, spasmodic and he regretted this later, saying he should have stayed on. He was employed several times, and up to acting ganger for seven years in the Queensland Railways at Kagaru. The railways offered better pay and conditions than most forms of labour for Aborigines at the time. This peak of employment for Aborigines in the NSW Railways, according to Moran, was from the 1960s onwards.

Another to find employment in the NSW railways was Raymond (Tiger) Kelly (1938-2007). He was a Dunghutti man from the Macleay region of the Mid-North Coast of New South Wales. He spent the first sixteen years of his life on the Bellbrook Mission near Kempsey. He joined the railways aged sixteen in Sydney but only worked there for a year. In 1973 Ray was the first Aboriginal person employed by the National Parks and Wildlife Service (Kelly in Maynard, 1999).

Kamilaroi man Norman Munro was quoted in the Railcorp NSW publication "Join Our Team", their Aboriginal Recruitment handbook (2006-7 Annual Report), saying, "My parents were railway workers. Dad was a Per-Way (*permanent way; the railroad track*) worker and Mum was a Gatekeeper. We have a family tradition of approximately 100 years with my two brothers Lyall and Bruce both working for the railways, as well as my three uncles. In the early days a lot of Aboriginal families could only get work on the railways - I travelled to Newcastle and got a job with the railways on the 16 February 1959; I've been here ever since. It was always my dream to work on the railways, just like my Dad". Apart from his story, no documentation exists about the employment of other family members. This reflects the hidden nature of Indigenous employment. They were assimilated into the rail system and so not documented as Indigenous workers. Hence, their contribution is not acknowledged in populist rail histories of the Hunter region.

This is also evident in Mckillop and Sheedy's book (2008) *Our Region, Our Railway - The Hunter and the Great Northern Railway 1857-2007*. Despite the above anecdotal accounts, there is no mention in the book itself of the Aborigines being employed on the railways. This work has no index mention of local Aborigines, in this case the Awabakal people.

John Maynard (2001), however, has written of Aboriginal workers in the Awabakal country around what is now Newcastle. They moved around the region seeking seasonal work and better opportunities for their families. In the early 1930s it was recorded that Aboriginal people had moved back into the Lake Macquarie district to work on the construction of railway lines. They lived in tents along the railway lines. Where these people had originally come from one can only speculate, Maynard says, but Aboriginal people of this period were prone and able to move great distances in their attempts to make a living.

Dr Greg Blyton has written "Sixteen pound hammers, fettlers and railway tents: the demographic relocation of Aboriginal people from rural to urban areas of New South Wales in the Assimilation Era 1950-1967" (Blyton, 2009). This paper has looked at the impact of assimilation policies on the lives of Aboriginal people in New South Wales through employment in the NSW Department of Railways. During this much later period hundreds of Aboriginal people were employed on the construction of railway track throughout many parts of New South Wales, which resulted in not only the relocation of Aboriginal employees from traditional rural settings to urban areas, but their entire families as well. This paper explored the nature of railway life for Aboriginal people and their families; the hard arduous labour of track laying, twelve hour working days swinging sixteen pound hammers, families living in railway tents alongside railway tracks and the eventual permanent relocation of these families from rural to urban areas.

In another paper, writing for Muswellbrook Shire, Blyton penned, "The Impact of Dispossession: Railway Tents, 14lb Hammers and Assimilation", Blyton wrote that employment in the railways was a major factor in causing Aboriginal people to come to the Upper Hunter Valley from places such as Scone, Aberdeen and Muswellbrook which were once the scene of numerous tents sited along the railway tracks. One Aboriginal man, Blyton commented, recalled that while there was discrimination against his people in the railways there was equal pay. He states: This man and other Aboriginal workers camped near Scone. There was still a stigma about Aboriginal people and they were fighting for just basic individual rights. In the railways they were treated equally for equal work. Aboriginal men often lived with their families in tents, which were hired from the Railway Department for around 5 shillings a week with optional extras such as wooden planks which served as floors and larger two room tents. There was no electricity and kerosene lanterns provided light at night, while food was cooked on fires. Despite employment in the white world Aboriginal people maintained a cultural sense of place and identity.

In the published version of his oral 2009 paper, Blyton (2013) expanded his focus from railway work to demographic movements of Aborigines in general, but included details of Aborigines and families moving to railway work. He also states that railway workers had equal pay well before the 1967 referendum (pages 180 to 182 especially).

In *Rivers and Resilience* (2009) Goodall and Cadzow write of Aboriginal people from the Salt Pan Creek area on the Georges River taking casual work on the suburban railway developments of the Great Depression era. Aborigines were routinely refused the new Unemployment Relief rations and work in many areas. Some of the men found work putting the railway line through to East Hills. A married man got two weeks on and one week off. A single man got one week on, three weeks off. This casual work is a contrast to Arabana options where many were ongoing employees.

Tasmania (settled by white people 1803)

Tasmania's first (1600 mm gauge) line opened in 1871 from Deloraine to Launceston and was converted to 1067 mm gauge in 1888. By this stage the Tasmanian Aborigines had long been decimated, the survivors rounded up, placed on Wybaleena on Flinders Island, reduced numbers further, been transferred back to southern Tasmania, and been officially written out of history. Lyndall Ryan (1996) in her seminal *The Aboriginal Tasmanians* does not even mention trains, rail or the like in her index. The more recent *Tasmanian Aborigines: A History since 1803* (2012) by the same author does not add to this information.

The renascent Tasmanian Aboriginal peoples probably number about 5,000 now but are more occupied with contemporary life where railways are much less significant than cars, trucks, buses and air transport.

Queensland (settled 1824; separate State 1859)

Aborigines are not mentioned as working on the railways in the official histories until the 1950s. There is massive concentration in the academic literature on the frontier wars, which were particularly bitter, and then the use of "Native Mounted Police" for decimating the survivors. Another population of non-European people, South Sea Islanders, were induced or kidnapped from the 1840s onwards to work on sugar plantations in Queensland, a practice called "blackbirding". This only ended after Federation in 1901.

Railways had arrived in 1865. Katie Maher (2012, 2013) states that Aboriginal people worked on construction of railway lines in NSW, Queensland, South Australia, Western Australia and the Northern Territory as packers and carriers, sleeper cutters and track layers. Women are said to have worked as laundresses and washerwomen. The women not infrequently married in and had children with non-Aboriginal railway workers. Documentary evidence for this remains very thin.

Torres Strait Islanders in Queensland and Western Australia

Leah Lui Chividzhe (2011) has written of the arrival and settlement of Torres Strait islanders recruited to work on the Queensland and West Australian mining railways from the 1950s. About ten per cent of the Torres Strait population left the islands and many worked on the railways. They hold a track laying record, from 1968, still celebrated.

I have spoken to one Torres Strait Islander man, Harold Matusia, who married into Arrernte and now lives in Aputula (the old Finke) on the old Ghan line.

Herb Shields (in Bitomsky and Mylne, 1995, p20) was reared in the Purga Mission near Ipswich. He was recruited aged 27 as a railway cleaner in which job he worked for four years. He must have been capable and ambitious as he qualified as a fireman thereafter. He became a train driver and locomotive inspector from the 1960s to the 1980s, albeit mostly working away from family and home. He remained a member of the Salvation Army for all of his life and was very actively involved in community activities. After a short illness he died in December 1999 aged 75 years. It was not until much later in his life that he sought out his own Aboriginality.

In his own quoted words, he cites other Aborigines working upon the Queensland rail: one at Maryborough, one at Mayne Junction and a few around Hughenden. Unfortunately no names are given nor do they appear elsewhere in the text.

Albert Holt (DOB 22nd November 1939) (2001, p108) born in Inala but reared in Cherbourg Mission worked on the railways as a fettler in the 1950s and asserts that "you just had to show up and the ganger could appoint you there and then". Later, like Paul Tanner of the Arabana, he worked in the Justice system, initially from 1995 as an Indigenous Police Liaison Officer, then helped establish the Murri Courts to reduce Indigenous incarceration and recidivism. Albert was State Finalist Senior Australian of the Year in 2010. In his birth suburb of Inala, a Community Housing development has been named the Uncle Albert Holt Terraces. He was President of Inala Wangarra, the local Aboriginal organisation, in 2013.

Dr George Skeene, a Yirrganydji Elder, born 1948, grew up on an Aboriginal Reserve in the Cairns area, and joined the railways in 1967 (Skeene, 2008). George's father, also called George, was already employed and was in the flying gang, which at that time was working strengthening the curves between Almaden and Forsayth in far north Queensland. George in his quoted words said there were already a lot of Aborigines and Torres Strait Islanders working on the railways. George's brothers, Mick, Rodney, Warren and Chris all later joined the railways. Sister Lesley married another flying gang member. One white person only was in that flying gang. Like Arabana they supplemented their diet by hunting and George records hitting a plains turkey with a rock flung from a section car. George was in the flying gang until 1983 when he moved into the carpenters' and plumbers' shop. After six years of this and when the Bitomsky and Mylne book was published in 1995, he was still working as a railway gardener. He retired in 2003 and published his autobiography *Two Cultures* in 2008. He was given an Honorary Doctorate by James Cook University in 2013 for his work researching his culture and artefacts. A significant basis for his later contributions to the community was laid by his railway involvement.

Geraldine Mate (2012) from the Railway Workshops Museum in Ipswich held an Exhibition in May 2012 called "I've Been Working on the Railroad" which subsequently toured Australia. In the accompanying brochure she summarised the Exhibition. Through the 1950s, 60s and 70s, she wrote, there were large scale developments of rail infrastructure across Australia. In the hot and dusty or wet and humid environments of the inland north, it was a common scene to find Torres Strait Islanders, Australian South Sea Islanders and Aboriginal people working long and hard in all weathers. This exhibition explored the little known railway stories of Aboriginal people, Torres Strait Islanders and South Sea Islanders and their contribution to the development of rail across Australia. Their stories are about their achievements, like the 1968 World Track Laying record set by predominantly Torres Strait Island gang, but also about so much more. The camp life, the realities of the work, the hardships, the separation from their land, islands and family and the opportunities and challenges of working on the railway. Today, the brochure concluded, Torres Strait Islanders, Aboriginal people and Australian South Sea Islanders work across the full spectrum of roles that make up railway activities.

There was just one mention of South Australian Arabana in this Exhibition, a photograph labelled "re-sleepering" but according to my Arabana informants. dealing with a derailment, as a Guard in uniform is present, which would not have been the case for a re-sleepering gang.

Western Australia (settled 1829; declared a separate state in 1890)

Given the Western Australia's vast size and small settler population, there has been a much higher dependence on Indigenous labour than in other States. As has been related in earlier chapters, the pastoral industry relied heavily on Indigenous workers. A similar reliance did not occur in the early development of the State's railways. In 1889, the privately built Great Southern Railway in the southwest corner of Western Australia was opened with subsequent economic growth to the regions along the line. The Government took over the line in 1896.

The wheat industry did not really get established until construction of railways allowed transport of the produce. A railway line had reached Coolgardie from Perth by 1896. Aboriginal dispossession and lack of involvement in this and later railways as builders or railway workers was the norm.

The Transcontinental Railway was built after Federation in 1901. The colonies of Australia were negotiating about Federation at the end of the 19th Century. The colony of Western Australia was encouraged to join this new nation, *inter alia*, by promise of a transcontinental railway, linking this isolated western region with the eastern colonies. Thus it is similar to the Canadian situation where British Columbia was promised a rail link in 1871 if it joined Canada in its federation. There were rail systems in the separate Australian States but a 1,996 kilometre gap existed in the system between Kalgoorlie in Western Australia and Port Augusta in South Australia.

On 17 October, 1917, two construction teams, in a remarkable surveying and engineering feat, one starting from Port Augusta and the other from Kalgoorlie, made an historic achievement, meeting to join the lines at what is now the tiny South Australian siding of Ooldea on the Nullarbor Plain. This was the longest railway ever built as a single project in Australia, taking five years to complete. It was constructed by men using the most basic tools – pick and shovel, carthorse and camel. Again land grants were given to the successful contractors – 12,000 acres (nearly 20 square miles) per mile of rail built. At 10:15 am on 25 October, 1917, the first eastbound passenger train, the Transcontinental Express, departed Kalgoorlie for Port Augusta.

The Transcontinental Railway had an adverse impact on the local Aboriginal people. Steam trains used huge amounts of water and Ooldea Soak was a major source. This spring, used for time immemorial by the local Aboriginal peoples, was run dry by the railway within a few years and was abandoned in 1926 as a water source.

Daisy Bates' *Passing of the Aborigines* (1926, Chapter 15, pp), written while she lived and worked at Ooldea, continued the myth of extermination: "So with the survey of the east-west railway began the extermination of the central native groups, not by the deliberate cruelty of the white man, but by the impossibility of amalgamating two such extreme races, Palaeolithic and 20th Century, and through the natives' ready, and even eager, adoption of the white man's vices.

As the construction proceeded, with a great influx of railway workers of all classes and nationalities, along 1,000 miles of previously uninhabited (!) country, they straggled in to the line in increasing numbers, drawn by the abundance of food-stuffs and the new fire-drink [Kala-gabbi] that made them "head no good." [Kooramba]. Each group through whose territory the line was passing saw its waters used up, the trees and bushes destroyed for firewood and fence-posts, and the whole country turned to strange uses. In their eagerness to "make the most of what they yet may spend," they did not know that they were bringing about their own annihilation. They thought that the train and its people would go away, and leave them the things to play with".

Daisy Bates set up her camp at Ooldea in 1919 and provided food, clothes and some medicine to the Aborigines who had gathered there. It was normally a temporary site for ceremonies, but the train induced more permanent habitation. Daisy stayed until 1934. David Burke says that the local Aborigines called the train "Maletna", great snake. The local Aborigines did not necessarily welcome Daisy Bates' presence. Later Ooldea became a Mission which only closed in 1952. Most inhabitants were moved to Yalata.

One of anthropologist Professor Peter Elkin's famous constructs is "intelligent parasitism", first voiced in the 1940s. This evolving idea suggests that Aborigines made use of the Transcontinental Railway in their own way. They made artefacts specifically for sale. They borrowed babies to appear more appealing to tourists and other train travellers. He saw this as a phase to, hopefully, intelligent appreciation then assimilation into settler culture (Elkin, 1951). He does not record Aboriginal workers upon the line, although there certainly were.

The "Tea and Sugar" ration cars ran from 1917 to 1996. Most of the film clips used in an instructional film called *On The Rails* about this train do not feature Indigenous Australians at all, or only incidentally. At this time, Indigenous people were considered an unimportant and insignificant element of Australian society. These films about railways praised European concepts like certain types of technology, industry, modernisation, progress, mineral exploitation and 'taming a savage and/or otherwise worthless land'. *On The Rails* was a celebration of the settler society's achievements, through the Transcontinental, and so Aborigines were excluded.

Mining Railways

I have covered the Torres Strait Islander involvement with laying tracks in the Queensland section, but Western Australia in the Pilbara was also the scene for such feats. Torres Strait Islander Mr Percy Maillie, one of whose sons married into Shirley Arbon's (nee Hodgson) family, was awarded a silver spike for his work on the northern railway lines of Western Australia.

Aboriginal people from South Australia did move to the East-West line, particularly after the closure of Killalpannina in Dieri country (see South Australian section), but information about these families is negligible.

Victoria (settled 1834; declared a separate state in 1851)

The first railway between Melbourne and Port Melbourne opened in 1854. The Melbourne and Suburban Railway Company's line from Princes Bridge railway station to Punt Road (Richmond) opened in 1859. In the same year the Geelong and Melbourne Railway Company opened its line from Melbourne to Geelong. Subsequently the Victorian Railways built new railways to connect farming and mining communities to the ports of Melbourne, Geelong and Portland. In 1862 lines reached the great gold rush towns of Bendigo and Ballarat. In 1864 a line was opened to the Murray River port of Echuca. In 1883 the first connection with another State's rail system was made when the North East line was completed to the New South Wales Government Railways station at Albury, requiring a break-of-gauge to New South Wales' 4 ft 8 1/2 in (1,435 mm) standard gauge Main Southern line. In 1887, Victorian Railways met South Australian Railways at Serviceton, with both systems using broad gauge.

Aboriginal Workers On The Victorian Railways

Gary Presland (2001) does not mention railways at all in his book on Aboriginal Melbourne. Richard Broome (2005) does not even mention the railways in his work on Aboriginal history in Victoria since 1800. The Koorie Heritage Trust has written to me and emphasised that Aboriginal people in Victoria after 1853 needed permits to travel anywhere including to work. This prohibition on movement was breached but hindered Aboriginal involvement in the railways or any other industry until much more recently.

Some people escaped this restriction. Lester Marks Harradine (1920-2010) was a Wotjobaluk man whose family lived on the Ebenezer Mission in North West Victoria. He was born in Bordertown South

Australia in 1920 but raised in Dimboola, and was interviewed for the Victorians at War Oral History Project (2001). He describes coming back from World War II and joining the railways in 1946 (aged 26). He trained as a fireman, which he did for five years, until qualifying as a locomotive driver in 1951. As far as I have been able to find out, he was the first qualified Aboriginal locomotive engineer. He played for the Australian Rules Football team of the railways when away from his home town of Dimboola. He stayed with the railways until retiring in 1980 aged 60. He helped establish Wurega Aboriginal Corporation and as a senior Wotjobaluk Elder he played a key role in establishing his family's claim in an historic 2005 Federal court decision to finally recognise native title rights and interests in the Wimmera.

Harridine's case was the exception rather than the rule. Given the restrictive legislation on Aboriginal movements in Victoria there was little opportunity for Indigenous peoples to gain work on the railways. Without this opportunity, Victoria's Aborigines remained largely segregated from the settler society and, consequently, were the most impoverished members of the community.

In a rather more sober event, in 2006 Yarra Yarra Tribal Elder Aunty Dot Peters (awarded basket and eel trap weaver) approached her local Returned and Services League to play the didgeridoo in honour of her father, who died when she was aged 12, on the Thai Burma Railway where he was a Prisoner of War of the Japanese (RSL website 2011; Yarra Ranges Museum, 2015). They did so and subsequently the RSL started proper recognition of all Indigenous service men and women.

Skipton Jacky Jacky and his tribe at the opening of the Beaufort Railway - clearly seen as well off the train of progress.

South Australia: (settled 1836 officially)
Ngarrindjeri lands
Goolwa - Port Elliot Railway

In 1851 the Harbour Commission set up by the Legislative Council at the urging of Lieutenant Governor Fox agreed to build a railway between Port Elliot and Goolwa at a cost of £20,000. It ended up costing £31,000 and wasn't finished until 1854. This was through Ngarrindjeri land and was just seven miles long. It was, by any measure, a bit of a disaster. It rarely made a profit as the trains carrying the goods travelled at about 10 km/h and had to be unloaded before the goods could be moved to the ships because the waters at Port Elliot were too shallow and the jetty was not long enough. After ten years of horse-drawn rail operation in which seven ships were wrecked off the coast, the port was moved to Victor Harbour instead.

First bridge and rail traffic across the Murray

The first bridge across the Murray was built at Murray Bridge (Pomberuk) in 1879 (also Ngarrindjeri land) - this largely replaced a number of ferry and punt crossings further down river. This bridge was initially for road traffic but in 1886 was finally ready to carry the railway line. This line extended to the South Australia/Victoria border. The bridge at Murray Bridge had a long genesis, having been proposed in 1864; the bridge spans were ordered from England, and received long before the final decision was made on where to place the bridge. By the early years of the 20th century road traffic was being delayed for several hours when the bridge was closed to allow trains to cross. A second bridge to carry the railway was proposed, and this was finally opened in November 1925.

From this area, Charles Runga appears in Geoffrey Manning's unpublished work: this Ngarrindjeri or Buandik man worked for 14 years in the South Australian Railways from 1874-1888 (The Public Service Review, 1896)."Another survivor was an Aborigine with the European name of Charles Runga and an 1888 newspaper report says: There is working on the Kingston to Naracoorte line... an Aboriginal named Charles Runga who has been on the line in the South East from its commencement, I believe. He had a few acres of land given to him where he built a cottage and until lately has been able to go home every evening to his wife and family. A few days ago this hard working industrious black received notice to leave in a fortnight... Now he is a workman equal to any on the line... One time they thought of making him a ganger and he ran the line daily for years... [Editor's note - There is no truth in the above statements but we have learned from another authority that the dismissal was made on economic grounds.] (*This is said to be derived from Geoffrey Manning's unpublished manuscript "A History of the Lower South East District of South*

Australia in the 19th Century")."

Other Aboriginal people than Arabana have been involved but probably mainly since the Second World War. Gladys Elphick (1904-1988), Kaurna/Ngadjuri descent, worked at the South Australian Railway's Islington Workshops (Australian Dictionary of Biography, 2007). She won an award for an invention improving the shop floor. She was awarded the MBE in 1971 in recognition of service to the Aboriginal community and South Australian Aborigine of the Year in 1984. She helped establish the South Australian Aboriginal Medical Service in 1977. A plaque for her is in the Jubilee 150 plaques along North Terrace, Adelaide.

Prominent activist Charles Nelson Perkins (1936-2000) was a stolen Arrernte child, mother Arrernte, father Kalkadoon from western Queensland. He was the first Aboriginal University graduate. He worked on the South Australian Railways (Perkins, 1975, Chapter 5, pp53-4; Read, 1990, p58) in the yard as a fitter and turner in the early 1960s, again with equal wages prior to the Equal Wages case in the later 1960s. He became an activist with the 1960s Freedom Rides and was instrumental in organising the Referendum in 1967 which led to Aborigines being counted in the Census for the first time and enabling the Federal Parliament to make laws about Aborigines. Perkins' working career as a tradesman in the railways supported the contention that unlike other industry sectors such as pastoralism, they provided a means for Indigenous peoples to both progress and eventually challenge the right of settler politicians to determine their lives.

Another Aboriginal man, Bobby Smith, is recorded by Ron Fitch as "my favourite Aborigine" and as being in charge of the Pedirka gang between 1949 and 1954 in his railwayman's memoirs. (Pedirka is about 100Km northwest of Oodnadatta; there was a train station there from 1928 to 1968). It is not clear which Aboriginal people

Bobby Smith belonged to. It is also unknown whether this is the same man as Robert Smith who with his brother William later established a successful Aboriginal labour hire company.

Adnyamathanha people worked on the railways, by now called ANR, Australian National Railways, their personnel records being found by this researcher in the State Records. Prominent is the Coulthard family, of whom eleven were employed in various trades and labouring jobs between 1960 and 1980. Vince Coulthard (born 1957) who worked with the Railways from 1975-1977 was State Finalist Australian of the Year in 2011. Other Indigenous families may well have had such employed by the ANR, but the personnel files do not always identify employees as Aboriginal.

Alec (Bumbolili) Kruger (DOB 25/12/1924; Mudburra people) was born on the banks of the Katherine River (Kruger and Waterford, 2007). He was removed from his family aged 3 1/2. Reared in institutions like the harsh Bungalow in Alice Springs, he then became a stockman in Arrernte country. He joined the Army in 1942, during World War II - equal pay for the first time. One of his colleagues in the Aboriginal Unit was Jack Hughes, of mixed Afghan and Aboriginal descent from the Marree area. After the War Alec and his Aboriginal friend Billy Goodall joined the railways at Hawley as fettlers together with his older brother George (ibid, pp151-3). He was only there for six months before moving on to other work. Much later he worked in Queensland pulling up and replacing sleepers on the Mt Isa to Townsville railway line (ibid, p216). He adds that he also worked as a fettler on the railway in Quiradella siding out of Djarra but "(T) hat was lonely work and I gave it away" (ibid, p233). In 1954 he again got work on the railways, working from Alice Springs down to Ooriminna. He worked with the Ah Chees, who are from Oodnadatta and some of whom identify as Arabana. Alec names other Aborigines on the line with him, Nugget Blackmore and Les Thompson. He says (ibid, p233) that "it turned out to be really good having a job at the railways". He stayed with the train line until the early 1960s when he got better money unloading copper ore trucks. Alec had many other roles until retiring and getting a Veteran's Pension after 1989, but never went back to rail. Alec was a claimant in the Stolen Generations High Court challenge in 1997 which was lost by the Aborigines. Alec has never been able to live and work in his own country.

Some other names appear in the Aboriginal Protection Board's minutes from 1954-7. Immanuel Mack was with the South Australian Railways working at Mile End in 1954. Thomas Henry Newchurch, married with eight children, from Point Pearce, was on the South Australian Railways at Blythe and successfully petitioned for furniture for his home on 3rd August 1955. Similarly Herbert Milera was given furniture while with the South Australian Railways at Black Rock on 6th June 1956. Showing how microscopic was the Aboriginal Protection Board's control is the subsequent annotation that the Board had approved his purchase of six rabbit traps (6th February 1957). Presumably a relative, Bryan Victor Milera, was given furniture while working with South Australian Railways (SAR) at Black Rock on 4th July 1956. William James Newchurch was with SAR at Koonibba on 17th November 1956. The Mileras and Newchurches have married into Arabana families and the names appear in Marilyn Hull-Stuart's genealogy (1998). Despite working for the railways, the lives of these workers were heavily regulated by the Board. Indeed, all purchases made by workers had to be approved by the Board.

Thus, in summary, there is work being carried out to expose the contribution of Aboriginal and Torres Strait Islander peoples to the railways across the nation of Australia and its constituent former colonies. The work is still partial but does seek to make visible the still often invisible Aboriginal and Torres Strait Islander continuing role as Australian workers and citizens. This book seeks to add to this increasing visibility and to help continue to break "the great silence". Arabana are unusual in that they were able to live and work on country. They were also recruited in larger proportionate numbers than any other group, thus advantaging the whole community not just individuals or individual families.

Darryl Thomas, Nukunu man

(conversation by telephone on 19th December 2016).

Darryl said he was born in 1949 and raised in Port Augusta. His grandfather Alexander Thomas worked on construction of the Ghan line (*possibly the section between Oodnadatta and Alice Springs between 1926 and 1929*). Grandfather was also a blacksmith upon the Commonwealth Railways. He told the family about his dismay when the other workers speared a large goanna with their crowbars. Father, a younger brother in his sibship, mainly worked upon the wharves, but Darryl recalls growing up to some extent in a railway house. Father was a carpenter's assistant on the railway, building houses at the camps. One Christmas, father and all his mates caught a Section Car home to spend time with families, but all were sacked thereafter. Father's five older brothers, upon return from WW2, started on the wharves, so father went there too.

A cousin worked in Alice Springs as a Fitter Railway Workshops (Refrigeration) for thirty years then spent the remainder of his working life at the Hospital.

Darryl himself left school and joined the Commonwealth Railways aged 15, in 1964, as a youth porter. He did leave, went to Western Australia with some shearers and became a shearer himself.

He rejoined the Commonwealth Railways in 1970. When he initially joined, he was given the task of clearing along old fence lines, working with the crane crew and yard gang. He said they finished the job in a week, and the boss said he had expected them to take a month; he was working too fast!

He worked in the Workshops. He did some office work and was also a fitter's assistant. He was up in Marree, the change of gauge station, quite a bit and knows some of the Arabana people I met and some who have died. The cranes for the piggyback freezer carriages not infrequently broke down and he helped the staff at Marree fix them.

Darryl mentioned Reg Dodd, nickname "Cheese" because of his wide smile, the Arabana man whose story appears in Chapter 5. He said many Arabana worked upon the Ghan line because it was "their way of life". They were there (that is, it was their country). They worked as everything from fettlers to shunters to station masters.

He became a train driver in 1973 and was Assistant Driver on the Ghan and on the Indian Pacific. He was Assistant Driver with the Queen's Silver Jubilee Train in 1977 (a great honour). He was due to take his final test when Australian National Railways was privatised in 1978 and he left. He had been based in Coober Pedy at the time, as the new Ghan line expanded north towards Alice Springs from Tarcoola.

One anecdote struck him as we talked. He was based then out at Tarcoola and there had been a derailment at Wilgena, west of Tarcoola itself. Men had been working nineteen hour shifts and came back to Tarcoola on Christmas Eve, very thirsty. The publican closed the pub. The local policeman came and said open up or I shall and serve all the drinks free. The publican opened the pub up.

He left for family reasons, having enjoyed the actual work and camaraderie of the Railways. His two children had been born and he wanted to spend more time with them. Privatisation did reduce the "family atmosphere". The Roster Clerk told his wife that Darryl was being moved to Alice Springs. He was out at Tarcoola at the time, eating Spam for Christmas dinner. Men with three day tucker boxes were being sent home but not him.

Darryl then moved to work at the Powerhouse where he stayed for the rest of his working life.

APPENDIX 2

SOME ARABANA RAIL WORKERS NAMES

Arabana Railway Workers
(National Australian Archive and SRSA, GRG52/1)
(* means spoken to for this work)

Amos, Dennis*
Amos, James
Amos, Mark
Barnes, Dudley*
Barnes, Robert
Buzzacott, Allan
Buzzacott, Hector
Buzzacott, Kenneth
Buzzacott, Kevin*
Buzzacott, Peter
Buzzacott, Thomas
Buzzacott, Trevor
Dodd, Arnold
Dodd, Bruce Allan
Dodd, Desmond
Dodd, Lennie
Dodd, Lionel Richard*
Dodd, Martha*
Dodd, Mervyn

Dodd, Percy
Dodd, Richard Donald
Dodd, Reginald*
Dodd, Ronnie
Gepp, Bob
Gepp, Dudley
Harris, Harold (junior, b 1947)
Harris, Harold (senior, b 1925)
Hodson, Edna Marie
Hodgson, John
Hull, David (aka Milera Kevin)
Hull, Glen
Hull, Roy
Hull-Stuart, Marilyn*
Kite, Esther
Stewart, Henry
Stewart, Joy
Stewart, Sydney
Strangways, Benjamin
Strangway, Brian William
Strangways, Cyril William
Strangways, Douglas
Strangways, Henry (Wapili)
Strangways, Herbert
Strangways, Leon Cyril
Strangways Leonard
Strangways, Sydney*

Strangways, Wilfred David*
Stuart, Dean*
Stuart, Laurie
Stuart, Lenard
Stuart, Locky
Stuart, Robert Anthony
Stuart, Rex
Tanner, Paul*
Warren, Arnold Ben
Warren, Arthur
Warren, Benjamin Russell
Warren, Clarrie (Clary)*
Warren, Clifford Gordon
Warren, David
Warren, Frank
Warren, Gordon
Warren, James
Warren, Jennifer
Warren, Keith
Warren, Margaret
Warren, Francis Maxwell
Warren, Roger
Warren, Ros
Warren, Ross*
Warren, Stan

(seventy-one people)

It is certain there were many more but records are just not adequate to identify them.

Laurie Stuart's sons, all of whom have worked with the railways. Left back. Len Stuart, Right back. Rex Stuart. Middle. Lawrence Stuart. Front. Robert Stuart and Dean Stuart.

(Photograph courtesy of the Stuart family ©)

TIMELINE

Time Immemorial - Arabana Inhabit The Western Kati Thanda/Lake Eyre Region

Dates chosen for Timelines reveal the predilections of the chooser. Even the idea of linear time is not the only construct: I may cite an argument about two ideas of Stephen Jay Gould's "Time's Arrow, Time's Cycle" 1987 for one. I let the reader work out my own views and prejudices from what is included and what is left out. I seek to have Ghan railway history woven into the timeline. Items in bold are directly about Arabana.

20,000 years - **Arabana around Kati Thanda** according to archaeologists Mulvaney and Kamminga, 1999 1500s (approx) -Macassan traders start visiting Northern Australia

Isaacs, 1980, esp. pp262-276

1788 - Sydney Cove settled by Europeans

1790-1802 - Pemulwuy, Eora people, resistance fighter, in Sydney area Willmot, 1987

1807 - Slavery abolished in British Empire (Abolition of the Slave Trade Act)

1825 - First commercial railway ran between Darlington and Stockton, Manchester, England, Ellis, 1976

1834 - Slavery abolished in England (British Slavery Abolition Act, 1834)

1836 - South Australia officially settled by Europeans, Taylor 2002

1839 - Edward Eyre sighted Lake Eyre (Eyre's Journals)

1849 - convict transportation abolished to Australia (except Western Australia where it continued to 1868), Chambers Encyclopaedia, 1895

1856 - Joseph Herrgott "discovered" mound spring named after him (Babbage's Journals)

1857 - "Indian Mutiny" – lack of railways contributed to reverses for British, Sharma, 2010

1858 - **Smallpox epidemic swept Arabana**, Kimber 1996

1861-5 - American Civil War – the first "railway war", Amsler, 2004

1863 - **Strangways sheep station established on Arabana land**

1864 - Samuel Stuckey, camel procurer, exculpated for murder of Dieri man (neighbours of Arabana)

1870-1872 - **Overland Telegraph Line built, including through Arabana land**, Thomson, 1999

1884 - **Central Australia Railway arrived in Hergott Springs, (Marree)**, Fuller, 1975

1891 - **Railway extended to Oodnadatta**, Fuller, 1975

1894-7 - Jandamara, Bunuba people, resistance fighter in the Kimberley

1901 - Australian colonies united to form Commonwealth of Australia Federation

- white Australia policy established by legislation

1911 - Commonwealth takes control of Northern Territory

1914-1918 - First World War

1914 onwards - **Arabana children being removed under legislation**

1918 - **"Spanish Flu" pandemic swept through Arabana,**

killing probably fifty per cent

1920 - **Dr Herbert Basedow Third Medical Relief Expedition examined Arabana**

1922 - **Finniss Springs Station re-established by Francis Dunbar Warren; about 150 Arabana lived there**

1924 - Australian Aborigines Progressive Association

1927 - Commonwealth assumed control of railway

1928 - Coniston (Northern Territory) massacre

1929 - Railway extended to Alice Springs

1938 - National Day of Mourning on Australia Day; publication of Capricornia

1939 - Finniss Springs UAM Mission established

1939-1945 - Second World War

1940s - **Henry Wapili Strangways, Alan Buzzacott and other Arabana people employed by Commonwealth Railways**

1945 - United Nations formed.

1946 - Pilbara Aboriginal pastoral workers strike

1947 - India gained independence

1954 - Atomic tests at Maralinga – **radioactive clouds drifted over Arabana**

1956 - beginning of NADOC (National Aborigines Day Observance Committee)

1958 - **death of Francis Dunbar Warren and closure of Finniss Springs Mission**, Marree Arabunna Tour pamphlet, 2011

1960 - **Reg Dodd, Arabana, employed as contract labour and, from 1966, train examiner through to 1986**

1962 - voting rights for Aboriginal people in Australia

1963 - assimilation policy articulated by Commonwealth, Wells, in Austin and Parry, 1998

1964 July - Donald Campbell set land speed record in Bluebird on Lake Eyre's dry salt bed

1965 - Charles Perkins, Arrernte people, first Aboriginal university graduate

- Commonwealth Arbitration and Conciliation Commission: Transcript of Case 830 of 1965:"Equal Wage Case"

1966 - Wave Hill walk-off

1967 - referendum allowed Aboriginal people to be counted in Australian census for first time and Federal Parliament to make laws regarding Aborigines

1971 - Neville Bonner, Jagera people, first Aboriginal Member of Federal Parliament

1972 - Aboriginal Tent Embassy established in Canberra

1974 - NADOC composed entirely of Aborigines for first time

1980 - Old Ghan route closed

1983 - first Aboriginal medical graduate, Helen Milroy, Palyku people from the Pilbara, pers. com. 1998

1987 - last train left Marree

1993 - Mabo High Court decision

1990s - **Native Title claims lodged for Arabana;** Arabunna Aboriginal Tours established;

- **Ularaka Arabunna Association established**

2010 - Lake Eyre floods

2011 - Helicopter crash with two ABC journalists and pilot killed near Cooper's Creek

- Lake Eyre Yacht Club refused permission by Arabana to sail on Lake

2012 - **22nd May: Native Title granted.**

2013 - **Leasehold over old Finniss Springs Station given to Arabana Aboriginal Corporation.**

Australia's North-South Transcontinental Railway, April 1928.
Putting the rails on the small collapsible tracks
(Photograph Courtesy of the State Library of South Australia [B 72167/5])

REFERENCES

Government Documents
Australian Dictionary of Biography. Various entries, including Luise Hercus, 'Warren, Arthur (1910–1989)', Australian Dictionary of Biography, National Centre of Biography, Australian National University,

State Records of South Australia:
-2000 *Ancestors in Archives.*
-*South Australian Railways, Preamble*, GRS42.
-*South Australian Railway Commissioner's Reports 1889 - 1975*, GRS306.
-*South Australian Railways Staff Register April 1853 – January 1913.* GRG/42/131.
-*South Australian Police Records, criminal history cards 1870-1999*, GRS/1060.

Books
Arabana Elders and Arbon, Veronica, -2010. *Wathili Family, Wibma Stories, Wadlhu Country.*

Attwood, Bain, -1989. *The Making of the Aborigines.* Allen & Unwin, Sydney.

Blainey, Geoffrey, -1967. *The Tyranny of Distance: how distance shaped* Australia's history. Sun Books, Melbourne.
-1975. *The Triumph of the Nomads: a history of ancient Australia.* Macmillan, South Melbourne.

Bourke, Colin, Bourke, Eleanor and Edwards, Bill (eds), -2004. *Aboriginal Australia (second edition)*. UQP, St Lucia.

Briscoe, Gordon, -1991. *A Social History of the Northern and Central Region of South Australia 1950-1979*. Unpublished MA Thesis, ANU; microfiche copy from NLA.

Chatwin, Bruce, -1988. *The Songlines*. Picador, London.

Davis, Michael, -2012. *Aboriginal Connections with Eveleigh*. Michael Davis Consultants.

Downes, Jim and Daum, Berthold, -1996. *The Ghan: from Adelaide to Alice*. Especially Chapter "Aborigines and the Ghan" by Dick Kimber. Lichtbild, Cromer Victoria.

Faith, N, -1993. *Locomotion: the railway revolution*. BBC Books, London

Farwell, George, -1950. *Land of Mirage: by camel through the Inland*. Angus & Robertson London.

Foster, Robert, Hosking, Rick and Nettelbeck, Amanda, -2001. *Fatal Collisions: the South Australian frontier and the violence of memory*. Wakefield Press, Kent Town.

Fuller, Basil, -1975. *The Ghan*. Rigby Adelaide.

Gale, Fay, -1964. *A Study in Assimilation: part-Aborigines in South Australia*. Libraries Board of South Australia, Adelaide. MA Thesis 1960.

Gammage, Bill, -2011. *The Biggest Estate on Earth: how Aborigines made Australia.* Allen & Unwin, Sydney.

Gibson, Jen in association with the Dunjiba Community Council Inc, -1988. *Some Oodnadatta Genealogies.* Department of Heritage and Planning.

Gibson, Jen and Shaw, Bruce (eds), -1990. *Wangkanyi: Aboriginal recollections of Oodnadatta.* Aboriginal Heritage Branch, Department of Environment and Planning, Adelaide.

Goodall, Heather and Cadzow, Jane, -2009. *Rivers and Resilience – Aboriginal people on Sydney's Georges River.* UNSW Press, Sydney.

Gregory, John Walter, 1906. *The Dead Heart of Australia: A Journey around Lake Eyre in the Summer of 1901-1902, with some account of the Lake Eyre Basin and the Flowing Wells of Central Australia.* John Murray, Albemarle St, London.

Hercus, Luise, -1994. *A Grammar of the Arabana-Wangkangurru Language of the Lake Eyre Basin, South Australia.* ANU Press Canberra.
-no date. Dictionary of Arabana language (4 files).

Hercus, Luise; Hodges, Flavia; Simpson, Jane (eds), -2009. *The Land is a Map.* ANU E Press, Canberra.

Hercus, Luise & Sutton, Peter, -1985. *The Assessment of Aboriginal Cultural Significance of Mound Springs in South Australia, Prepared by L Hercus & P Sutton in association with Kinhill Stearns for the Olympic Dam Project, December 1985, 75 pages.*

Hull-Stuart, Marilyn, -1998. *My Child, My Family.* Europa Press.

Jennings, Reece Ian, -1973. *W.A.Webb, South Australian Railways Commissioner, 1922-1930. A political, economic and social biography.* Nesfield Press, North Plympton.

Jessop, William, -1862. *Flindersland and Sturtland, or The Inside and Outside of* Australia, in 2 volumes.

Richard Bentley, New Burlington St, London. R Clay, Son and Taylor, Bread Hill Street, London.

Jones, Philip, -2007. *Ochre and Rust: artefacts and encounters on Australian frontiers.* Wakefield Press Adelaide.

Kerwin, Dale, -2010. *Aboriginal Dreaming Paths and Trading Routes: the colonisation of the Australian economic landscape.* Sussex Academic Press, Eastbourne.

Kidd, Rosalind, -1996. Aborigines and the Ghan Train in Downes, Jim. *The Ghan* pp 47-49. Lichbild P/L, Cromer Victoria.

Kunoth, Charles, -1988 (ed Shaw, Bruce). *Muloorina Heritage: memoirs 1908 – 1930.* Typescript, unpublished, South Australian State Library.

Litchfield, Lois, -1983. *Marree and the Tracks Beyond in Black and White.* Self-published.

Lockyer, Paul, -2011. *Lake Eyre: a journey through the heart of the continent.* ABC Books.

Luke, Monte, -1997. *Riders of the Steel Highways: the history of Australia's Commonwealth Railways, 1912-1975*. Privately printed, Port Augusta.

Mattingley, Christobel and Hampton, Ken (eds), -1988. *Survival in Our own Land: Aboriginal experiences in 'South Australia' since 1836*. Hyde Park Press, Adelaide.

McBryde, Isabel, -1987. Goods from another country: exchange networks and the people of the Lake Eyre Basin, in Mulvaney, J. and P.W. White (eds), *Australians to 1988, vol. 1 of Australians, A Historical Library*, 25373, Fairfax, Syme and Weldon, Broadway, p253.

McDouall Stuart, John, -1858, 1959, 1860, 1861, 1862. The Journals of John McDouall Stuart.

McFarlane, Ingereth and Hannah, Mark, -2007. *Transgressions: critical Australian Indigenous histories*. Chapter 3, 35-62 ANU E Press, Canberra.

McGrath, Ann, Huggins, Jackie, Saunders, Kay, eds., Aboriginal Workers, special edition of *Labour History*, November 1995.

McGregor, Russell, -1996. Intelligent Parasitism: A.P. Elkin and the Rhetoric of Assimilation. *Journal of Australian Studies*, 20 (50-51). pp. 118-130.

Marshall, Paul (ed), 2 -2011 (first edition 1989). Raparapa: stories from the Fitzroy River *drovers*. Magabala Books, Broome.

Morison, Ian Warren, -2012. *The Warrens: "Springfield" & Beyond*. Self-published by author, 22 Darling St, Barton, ACT 2600.

Newell, Brian R, -2000. *Following the Old Ghan Railway Line 1878-1980.* Custom Press, Adelaide.

Newland, Simpson, -1887. *The Far North Country.* Burden and Bonython, Adelaide. -1888. *Our Waste Lands.* Burden and Bonython, Adelaide.
-1902. *Land-Grant Railway Across Australia: the Northern Territory of the state of South Australia as a field for enterprise and capital.* S.A. Government, Adelaide.
-1926. *Memoirs of Simpson Newland.* F.W.Preece and sons, Adelaide.

Pascoe, Bruce, -2014. *Dark Emu: Black Seeds : agriculture or accident?* Magabala Books, Broome.

Paterson, Alistair, -2008. *The Lost Legions: culture contact in colonial Australia.* Altamira Press London.

Pearce, Andrew, - no date. *The Land of Sunburnt Babies.* Lush, Adelaide.
- no date. *Brown Boys and Boomerangs.* United Aborigines Mission.
Plowman, Robert Bruce,
-1933, *The Man From Oodnadatta.* Angus and Robertson, Sydney.
-1935. *Camel Pads.* Angus and Robertson, Sydney.

Rajkowski, Pamela, -1987. *In the Tracks of the Camelmen.* Angus & Robertson North Ryde.

Raynes, Cameron, -2002. *"A Little Flour and A Few Blankets": an administrative history of Aboriginal affairs in South Australia.* Government of South Australia, Adelaide.

Rowley, Charles Dunford, -1970. *The Remote Aborigines.* Pelican, Sydney.

Rowse, Tim, -1998. *White Flour, White Power: from rations to citizenship in Central Australia.* Cambridge University Press, Cambridge.

Shanahan, Frank (ed) and Bridges, Philippa, -1996. *Oodnadatta Walkabout: memoir of a 1924 camel trip.* Frank Shanahan, Seacliff.

Shaw, Bruce, -1990; ed. Dallwitz, John. *Horrie Simpson's Oodnadatta.* Oodnadatta Progress Association.
-1995. *Our Heart is the Land: Aboriginal reminiscences from the Western Lake Eyre basin.* Aboriginal Studies Press, Canberra

Simpson, Horace ND, *-Memoirs Of A Train Driver:* unpublished

Stevens, Frank, - 1974. Aborigines in the Northern Territory Cattle Industry. ANU Press, Canberra.

Stewien, Ron, -2007. *A History of the South Australian Railways Volume 1: the early years.* Australian Railway Historical Society, Melbourne 28.

Strangways, Brian, -2011. *You Have to Survive Somehow.* Nyiri Publications, Murray Bridge.

Thomson, Alice,
-1999. *The Singing Line: the story of the man who strung the telegraph across Australia and the woman who gave her name to Alice Springs.*Chatto & Windus London.

Weidenbach, Kristin, -2003. *Mailman of the Birdsville Track: the story of Tom Kruse.* Hodder Sydney.

Articles

Dodd, Reginald and Gibson, Jen, -1989, *Learning Times: An Experience of Arabana Life and Mission Education.* Aboriginal History Vol 13, 81-93.

Hercus, Luise, -2009. *Murkarra, a landscape nearly forgotten: the Arabana country of the noxious insects, north and northwest of Lake Eyre.* In Aboriginal Placenames: naming and renaming the Australian landscape, ed Koch, Harold and Hercus, Luise, Chapter 11, 257-272. ANU epress.
-1971. *Arabana and Wangkangurru Traditions.* Oceania, Vol 42, No 2 (December 1971), 94-109.

Kimber, Richard, -1988. *Smallpox in Central Australia: evidence for epidemics and postulations about impact.* Australian Archaeology 27, (December), 63-68.

McBryde, Isabel, -2000. *Travellers in storied landscapes: a case study in exchanges and heritage.* Aboriginal History, Vol 24, 152-174.

Maher, Katie, -2012. *We were all involved in the line: Making Visible the History of Aboriginal Workers on Rail.* Unpublished paper delivered at Australian Historical Association Conference.

Oastler, John Churchill, -1908. Administration of Justice in the Back Blocks. *The Honorary Magistrate* 205-209.

www.ingramcontent.com/pod-product-compliance
Lightning Source LLC
Chambersburg PA
CBHW071838230426
43671CB00012B/1991